MW01251834

DIM SUM KITCHEN

DIM SUM KITCHEN

PAGE ONE

DIM SUM KITCHEN
© 2009 PAGE ONE PUBLISHING PTE LTD

Published in 2009 by
Page One Publishing Pte Ltd
20 Kaki Bukit View
Kaki Bukit Techpark II
Singapore 415956
Tel: [65] 6742-2088
Fax: [65] 6744-2088
enquiries@pageonegroup.com
www.pageonegroup.com

Editor: Melody Tan
Assistant editor: Lee Xiaohui and Crystal Lee
Designer: Beverly Chong and Feng Dexian

ISBN 978-981-275-178-2

Printed and bound by Dami Editorial & Printing Services Co. Ltd.

Contents

A Short History of Chinese Dim Sum

The Chinese have been eating dim sum since 770 B.C. "Dim sum" originally meant "snacks for when you're hungry". We have no way of knowing what was China's oldest form of dim sum, but we do know that the poet Qu Yuan was already writing about it 2500 years ago. His poem "Calling the Soul" refers to 3 kinds of snacks – a cake made of honey and rice flour, a soft cookie with honey, and a sugary fried pretzel.

In the Song dynasty, a female writer named Wu coined the term "tianshi" in her work "Home Cooking", which literally translates to sweet dim sum. In the later Yuan dynasty, "The Collection of Home Essentials" by an anonymous author also included the term "congshi", which means small pastries. From literature such as these, we learnt that what we call "dim sum" had evolved from the rich culture of ancient snacks.

In the Ming and Qing dynasties, cooking techniques saw huge improvements, making dim sum production more complex and its culture more mature. From intricate palace dim sum, East-meets-West Huaiyang dim sum and spicy Sichuanese dim sum, to rustic Northeastern dim sum and refreshing Cantonese dim sum; every region had its own style. Because of the physical size of China, every region had its own foodstuffs, climate, culture and customs, and therefore every kind of dim sum had its unique cooking processes and tastes.

Dim sum from the North and South varied greatly in taste and culture. Northern dim sum was more of a staple while in its Southern counterpart, it was a snack. Northern dim sum had a longer history. In the North, it was part of courtly receptions, whereas in the South, it was meant to be enjoyed at leisure, most of the time next to scenic lakes. As the produce and local tastebuds varied, Southern dim sum was sweet and Northern dim sum savoury, while Eastern dim sum had a lighter taste and Western dim sum spicy.

Other than differing regions, every season also had its specialty dim sum – puffs in spring, cakes in summer, cookies in autumn and sweets for the winter.

Speaking of traditional dim sum culture, it is impossible not to discuss the Southern "zouca", translated to "breakfast tea", at length. Offering tea to guests has long been a standard etiquette, a way of expressing the host's welcome and friendship. The tea is accompanied by plates of delicious dim sum, making the drinking process entertaining and also brings a rarefied form of pleasure.

In Guangxi and Guangdong, "zouca" has long been a way of life. To a certain extent, "zouca" does not merely sate hunger, but also a way of enjoying particular settings, leisure times and atmospheres. "Zouca" is most commonly taken at around nine in the morning, and at this time, tea houses are already bustling.

"Zouca" dim sum encompasses all sorts of cooking processes like steaming, pan-frying, deep-frying and many more. Not only does the food need to be fresh, it also has to excel equally in its presentation, fragrance and taste. The more varied the dim sum the better, thus most tea houses offer at least 40 types of dim sum, with the larger establishments serving as many as 80. Even till today, new varieties of dim sum continue to evolve, relegating tea to just a supporting role in "zouca".

As China's economy takes off, the tradition of consuming dim sum becomes more and more common in people's lives.

Dim sum has the following characteristics:
• It is meant to be eaten as a snack before or after meals, unless it forms part of a banquet.
• It is mainly made of rice, flour and rice flour, but there are also other types of dim sum made from beans, dairy products and animal parts.
• Dim sum made in restaurants, eateries and roadside stalls are meant to be served hot, while factories mainly produced cold dim sum that is meant to be consumed with hot drinks.
• There are no clear distinctions between dim sum and snacks, and the differences also vary by regions, making for a rather confusing situation.

Basic Tools for Making Dim Sum

Kneading

The rolling pin is a cylinder with a diameter of about 2 to 3 cm and is usually made of wood. It is used to flatten the dough and is indispensable in the hand-making process of dim sum. There are several types of rolling pins:

• Normal rolling pin – This can be used to roll dough for noodles, wonton skins, pau skins, and dumpling skins, just to name a few.

• Hollow rolling pin – The center is hollow all the way through, leaving space for a thin stick to be inserted as the handle. Big hollow rolling pins are used to roll larger pieces of dough, e.g. for twisted rolls, whereas smaller hollow rolling pins are mainly used to prepare the dough for siew mai.

• Tapered rolling pin – It is thicker in the middle and slightly thinner at the ends, and is mainly used to roll the dough for dumplings and siew mai.

Cleaning

Dough scraper – It is usually made of copper, aluminum, iron or plastic, and is used to scrape dough, knead flour and cut up rolls of dough.

Brush – Made of ears of sorghum or broom corn millet with the grain removed and tied together. It looks like a small broom and is used to sweep flour off the working surface.

Mini-dustpan – Woven out of rattan, willow branches or bamboo splints, flour can be swept into it, and it can also be used to scoop up flour.

Moulding

Moulds – Made of wood, copper, iron, aluminum or other materials. They vary in shapes and sizes according to their purposes. They mostly have images or words carved into them, like the moulds for mooncakes and cakes.

Chops – Wooden chops with carved images or words are used to imprint carvings on dim sum.

Stamps – Made of different materials in shapes of birds, flowers or insects.

Forceps – Mainly used to shape and cut pastry into special shapes.

Small scissors – Used to trim pastry into fancy shapes.

Cooking

Strainer – A metal ladle with a handle that has many even-sized holes to drain out the oil and water in food.

Webbed ladle – Its scoop is made of stainless steel or metal threads woven together and is used to drain the oil from deep-fried food.

Slice – A big metal spatula used to flip food when frying or baking.

Metal chopsticks – Can be used during deep-frying to flip and remove food.

Making Stuffings and Seasonings

Knife – Used to cut noodles and dice fillings.
Whisk – Used to stir and beat eggs and fillings.
Baking brush – Mainly used to brush colour onto pastries.
Flat brush – Used to brush oil onto pastries.

Cutlery

Dim sum can be served in plates, saucers and bowls of all sorts of designs and patterns. They can be made of wood, bamboo, porcelain, glass or metal, though porcelain is the most widely used. Choosing the appropriate cutlery will make your dim sum even more visually attractive.

Common Seasonings and Ingredients

Common Herbal Condiments
Cinnamon stick, star anise, fennel, spring onion, grain of paradise (guinea grain), clove, nutmeg, cinnamon, ginger, garlic, peppercorn and preserved mandarin orange peel.

Common Seasonings
Salty – All types of table salt, sweet sauce, dry sauce, fermented bean sauce, red soy sauce, white soy sauce, shrimp roe soy sauce, dried mushroom soy sauce, fermented black bean sauce, soy cheese, etc.

Sweet – White sugar, brown sugar, rock sugar, honey, malt sugar, artificial sweetener, etc.

Sour – Rice vinegar, smoked vinegar, white vinegar, lemon juice, haw juice, plum sauce, ketchup, juice from pickled cabbages, etc.

Bitter – Almonds, preserved mandarin orange peel, coffee, tea leaves, etc.

Umami – MSG, chicken essence, prawn oil, fermented prawn sauce, oyster sauce, fish sauce, crab sauce, razor clam oil, shrimp, crabs, ham, fresh soup, etc.

Spicy – Chilli powder, chilli oil, dried chilli, dipped chilli (fish chilli), chilli sauce, spicy thick broad-bean sauce, wasabi, ginger, garlic, whole peppers, pepper etc.

Fragrant – Rice wine, sweet rice wine, distillers' grains, distillers' grains oil, cinnamon sticks, cardamom, sesame oil, osmanthus, sesame seeds, peanuts, ground walnuts, food flavourings, etc.

Tongue-numbing – peppercorns, peppercorn oil, etc.

Common Dips
Rice vinegar, red vinegar, white sugar, soy sauce, spicy soy sauce, sweet noodle sauce, and other dips that vary by region.

Common Ingredients
Meat – Pork, beef, chicken, mutton, seafood.

Vegetables – Chinese cabbages in winter, carrots, celery, chives in spring, winter melons in summer, etc. They can be mixed with meat to make fillings.

Beans – Used to make bean paste, e.g. red beans, green beans, peas, etc.

Dry fruits and nuts – Red dates, walnuts, sesame, peanuts, melon seeds, longans, lychees, almonds, etc.

Fruits – Commonly used fruits include peaches, mandarin oranges, apples, pineapples, pears, waxberries (bayberries), etc.

Flowers – Used to enhance fragrance and colour. The most commonly used flowers are rose, osmanthus, jasmine, white michelia, etc.

Gels – Gels used to make dim sum include agar and gelatin.

Common Dim Sum Skins
How to make dumpling skins:

Kneading the flour – The most common way is to use 4 parts wheat flour, and add about 1 part water. After kneading the flour into a smooth lump, cover with a wet cloth and leave for about 15 minutes, giving the water time to soak through the flour. The more water you use, the softer the dough, which makes it easier to wrap it around the filling, though the dough will have a higher tendency of breaking when cooked. If lesser water is used, the dough will be harder and tougher to roll and wrap. For the best texture, the dough should be slightly tough.

Rolling the dough – Place the soaked dough on the counter and shape it into long sticks with diameters of about 2 to 3 cm each. Cut the sticks into shorter rolls of about 1 to 2 cm long. Using a rolling pin, press the rolls into flat circles of about 7cm in diameter. The circles should be about 1cm thick, but slightly thicker in the middle than around the edges. The thick middle ensures that the filling will not leak out, and the thin edges are easier to bite into. When you roll the dough, remember to sprinkle some dry flour onto the counter to prevent the dough from sticking.

As rolling the flour can be quite time-consuming, many shops today sell machine-made dumpling skins. When using these skins, you usually need to wet your hands before wrapping them around the fillings.

How to make wonton skins
Place wheat flour into a container, add in water as above and hand-knead into dough. Cover with a wet cloth and leave for about 15 minutes, giving the water time to soak through the flour. Roll the dough into flat pieces with an even thickness of about 0.2cm, then cut it into trapeziums with a base length of about 10cm, and you have wonton skins.

How to make pau skins
Add about 2 parts flour, 1 part warm water and moderate amounts of old dough or yeast powder, and knead into soft rolls of dough. Keep in a warm place to ferment until it becomes twice its original size.

Then add in a pinch of baking soda, and mix evenly throughout. Cover with a wet cloth and leave for about 15 minutes, giving the water time to soak through the flour. This can be used to make the skins for all kinds of paus or buns.

How to Cook Dim Sum

Steaming
Place moulded raw food into steamers and over a pot of water. Put the fire on high. The boiling water will produce steam that will cook the food. This method of cooking is known as steaming, and the outcome is known as "shi" or "steamed food".

Boiling
The moulded raw food is thrown into a pot of water, and is cooked with the convection currents in heated water. This method is widely used, especially for flour-based and rice-based products.

Pan-frying
Use less oil and a flat-bottomed saucepan. How much oil to use depends on the outcome desired, but it is usually just a thin layer brushed on the bottom and should not be more than half the thickness of the desired product. There is also another type of frying, which uses both water and oil, where some water is added to produce steam. The outcome is then crispy in parts and soft in others.

Deep-frying
This method requires a big pot full of oil. The desired product should be totally immersed in the oil with enough space to move around. After the oil is heated up, the products are lowered into the pot one by one. They should be evenly fried till done and can usually be removed when they turn golden-brown.

Grilling
The moulded raw food is placed in a flat-bottomed saucepan, which is placed on fire. The food is cooked through the heat that is transmitted through the metal pan. When grilling, both sides of the product repeatedly come in contact with the bottom of the pan till done, and thus, grilled products are mostly crispy on the outside and soft on the inside. They will look yellowish-brown like a tiger's hide, or, if brushed with oil, golden-brown.

Baking
Food is cooked at high temperatures in various sorts of ovens. Baked dim sum have the following characteristics including high temperatures, even heating, bright coloring, appealing shapes to name a few. They can have varied flavours or can be crispy on the outside and soft on the inside, both of which are very tangy to the bite.

蒸
点

STEAMED
DIM SUM

鮮肉小籠 (xian1 rou4 xiao3 long2)
MEAT DUMPLINGS

Meat dumplings are a tradition of Shanghai dim sum and of them the most renowned are dumplings from Nanxiang town. They are known for their thin and translucent skins, abundant and juicy fillings, as well as their fresh and intense flavour.

Ingredients

• wheatflour	650g	• salt	10g
• pork thigh	600g	• juice from ginger	5g
• pork gelatin (without skin)	350g	• juice from shallot	5g
• soy sauce	30g	• sesame oil	15g
• MSG	3g		

Preparation

1. Dice the pork thigh finely (or use a blender). Add in the salt, soy sauce, MSG, sesame oil, juice from ginger and shallot, and mix well. Then add in finely diced gelatin, and mix them well to make the filling. Separate into 100 portions for use later. 2. Set aside about 50g of the flour for dusting your hands and mix the rest with warm water. Leave the mixture for a moment before rolling it into long sticks. Separate into 100 portions. Using a rolling pin, roll them into flat circles of about 5cm in diameter, thicker in the middle. 3. Put the filling in the middle of the circle, and wrap it up, making about 13 folds in each skin. If preferred, leave a small hole in the middle, through which you can see the filling. 4. Place the dumplings neatly in the steamer, and steam on high heat for about 10 minutes.

Variations

CRAB ROE DUMPLINGS – Prepare the basic dumpling, mixing crab roe well into the filling.
PRAWN DUMPLINGS – Prepare the basic dumpling, mixing diced prawns well into the filling.
"THREE TASTES" DUMPLINGS – Prepare the basic dumpling, using diced chicken, bamboo shoots and prawns for the filling.

CUTTLEFISH MEAT DUMPLINGS Prepare the basic dumpling, mixing diced cuttlefish well into the filling.
MUSHROOM MEAT DUMPLINGS – Prepare the basic dumpling, mixing diced shiitake mushrooms well into the filling.

回鍋肉夾餅 (hui2 guo1 rou4 jia2 bing3)
DOUBLE-COOKED PORK IN BUNS

Double-cooked pork is a Sichuan favourite. It is spicy and salty, soft and rich without being greasy. Pairing buns with the pork is a divine combination and very popular with diners.

Ingredients

• flour	300g	• soaked and diced chilli	2g
• yeast powder	20g	• sweet fermented flour paste	3g
• fatty pork with skin	400g	• soy sauce	2g
• chopped green spring onions	10g	• sugar	5g
• shallots	3g	• MSG	2g
• coriander	3g	• starch	2g
• sliced ginger	2g	• yellow wine	4g
• ground spring onions	2g	• chilli oil	3g
• spicy broad-bean paste	5g	• vegetable oil	30g

Preparation

1. Mix the flour and yeast powder with warm water and leave for 2 hours. When you see air bubbles in the dough, hand-knead and separate into portions weighing 50g each. Press them into 1cm-thick circles, and bake in a pan (without oil) till the surface is slightly hard. 2. Place the pork in boiling water till it is just cooked, then cut into thin slices, leaving the skin on. Heat a wok and stir-fry the pork till the fatty parts seep out. Then add the spicy broad-bean paste, chilli, ginger, shallots, ground spring onion and sweet fermented flour paste, and stir-fry till a fragrance arises. Add in the soy sauce, chilli oil, sugar, MSG and fry, mixing them well. Put in the coriander and chopped spring onions just before removing from the wok and placing in a plate. 3. Cut open the buns and stuff the filling in, then steam for 10 minutes and serve.

Variations

CHAR SIEW IN BUNS – Dice char siew pork, stir-fry for a while, then add honey and blend to make the filling.

FISH-FLAVOURED PORK IN BUNS – Cut pork, bamboo shoots and black Jew's ear into thin strips and stir-fry. Add condiments like sugar, vinegar and salt, then thicken with cornstarch for the filling.

ONION AND MUTTON IN BUNS – Fry onion and mutton on high heat for the filling.

FRIED PORK IN BUNS – Fry some finely diced pork for the filling.

SPICY CHICKEN IN BUNS – Fry diced chicken on high heat, then add chilli sauce and fry for the filling.

果脯松糕 (guo3 pu3 song1 gao1)
DRIED FRUIT IN SPONGE CAKE

Sponge cakes are a Cantonese snack with a rich history. Soft yet bouncy, they are light yellow, small and spongy throughout. The most common of these are corn cakes, which are popular for their golden colour.

Ingredients
- corn flour   200g
- flour   100g
- eggs   2
- sugar   20g
- condensed milk   20g
- cheese powder   20g
- baking powder   10g
- assorted dried fruits

Preparation
1. Mix all the ingredients, except the fruits, together. Add water to make a paste, taking care to avoid air bubbles in the paste. Leave for a few minutes to let it rise. 2. Line the moulds with paper, pour the paste in and sprinkle the fruits on top. Steam on high heat till they come cleanly out of the moulds.

Variations
PLUM BLOSSOM CAKES – Wrap sweet red bean paste into the middle of the cakes, and then put it in a mould shaped like a plum blossom. Sprinkle red and green strips of melon, and steam on high heat till done.

三色包 (san1 se4 bao1)
TRI-COLOURED BUNS

In this creative take on buns, the different colours signify different fillings.
The buns are appealing in colour and varied in taste.

Ingredients

•	wheat flour	500g	• beef	400g
•	corn flour	300g	• carrots	200g
•	spinach	500g	• onions	150g
•	yeast	20g	• soy sauce	30g
•	pork thigh	600g	• MSG	5g
•	cabbage	400g	• salt	20g
•	celery	500g	• sesame oil	30g

Preparation

1. Dice the pork, beef, carrots and onions finely. Blanch the cabbage and celery and dice finely. 2.
Prepare 3 kinds of fillings – pork with cabbage, pork with celery and beef, carrots and onions.
3. Mix soy sauce, MSG, salt and sesame oil into all the 3 fillings. 4. Make 3 kinds of dough – plain
flour, corn flour mixed with flour and juice from the spinach mixed with flour 5. Add yeast to all 3,
and wait till they rise before wrapping in different fillings. Mix and match the fillings and skins as
you wish. 6. Steam on high heat for 10 minutes and serve.

Variations

BEEF ONION BUNS – Use diced beef and onions
as the filling.
PORK BUNS – Use finely diced pork as the filling.
MUTTON BUNS – Use finely diced mutton as the
filling, adding cooking wine to remove any stench.
"THREE TASTES" BUNS – Use diced chicken,
bamboo shoots and mushrooms as the filling.

蒸糯米肉园 (zheng1 nuo4 mi3 rou4 yuan2)

STEAMED GLUTINOUS MEATBALLS

This dish is made by rolling meatballs in glutinous rice. The savoury meat and sweet rice make for an exquisite combination.

Ingredients

• glutinous rice	80g
• diced pork filling	200g
• starch	40g
• salt	5g
• dark soy sauce	8g
• pepper	a pinch
• sesame oil	3g
• char siew sauce	5g
• diced garlic	8g
• diced ginger	5g

Preparation

1. Wash the glutinous rice and soak for 12 hours, then drain. 2. Add the starch, salt, dark soy sauce, pepper, sesame oil, char siew sauce, diced garlic and diced pepper into the pork filling. Stir in a single direction with chopsticks, till the filling comes up in strips when you lift the chopsticks. 3. Shape the filling into meat balls and roll them in the glutinous rice till the meatballs are completely covered. Steam on high heat till done.

Variations

PORK FLOSS AND GLUTINOUS RICE BALLS – Add pork floss to the filling.
MOULDED DRIED VEGETABLE AND GLUTINOUS RICE BALLS – Add diced moulded dried vegetables to the filling.

SALTED EGG AND GLUTINOUS RICE BALLS – Steam salted duck eggs, grind the egg yolks and add into the filling.
FRIED DOUGH STICK AND GLUTINOUS RICE BALLS – Add diced fried dough sticks (you tiao) to the filling.

鲜肉大蒸饺 (xian1 rou4 da4 zheng1 jiao3)
STEAMED PORK DUMPLINGS

Steamed Pork Dumplings is a very common dim sum dish. The dumplings
are soft and sticky, while the filling is infused with a tasty sauce.

Ingredients

•	wheat flour	600g	• MSG	3g
•	lean and fatty pork	600g	• soy sauce	35g
•	pork gelatin (without skin)	300g	• cooking wine	15g
•	winter bamboo shoots (covering removed)	60g	• juice from shallots	10g
			• juice from ginger	10g
•	shrimp roe	6g	• sesame oil	35g
•	salt	6g		

Preparation

1. Clean the pork and dice into cubes of about 0.3cm in length. 2. Wash the winter bamboo shoots
and blanch in boiling water till just cooked. Drain and dice finely. 3. Dice the gelatin till it becomes
a paste. 4. Add the pork into a deep bowl. Add water and beat till it becomes sticky. Then add
cooking wine, soy sauce, salt, MSG and juice from shallot and ginger and mix. 5. Add the gelatin
paste, bamboo shoots, shrimp roe and sesame oil, and mix everything well to make the filling. 6.
Add 7 parts hot water into the flour, till the flour resembles snowflakes floating on the water. Once
it has cooled, add in 3 parts cold water and knead into a dough. Shape the dough into long sticks
and separate into portions weighing about 40g each. Flatten and knead them into circles, wrap the
filling in to achieve a moon-like shape. 7. Steam on high heat for about 10 minutes and serve.

Variations

SHRIMP DUMPLINGS – Add diced shrimps
into the pork filling.
CHICKEN DUMPLINGS – Work chicken into a
paste, wrap in the skins and steam.
SALTED EGG PORK DUMPLINGS – Grind the
yolks of salted eggs and add into the pork filling.

BEEF DUMPLINGS – Work beef into a paste,
wrap in the skins and steam.
MUSHROOM PORK DUMPLINGS – Add
diced mushroom and celery into the pork filling.

三色糕 (san1 se4 gao1)

TRI-COLOURED CAKES

You can mix and match the 3 flavours any way you like. These brightly coloured cakes look adorable and irresistable.

Ingredients

- flour   300g
- yeast   10g
- matcha (green tea) powder   20g
- cocoa powder   20g
- milk   50cc
- soft sugar   80g
- walnuts   15g
- red beans   15g
- raisins   15g

Preparation

1. Divide the flour into 3 portions, mixing matcha powder, milk and cocoa powder into them respectively. Then add yeast and soft sugar. **2.** Mix the 3 kinds of flour and leave for 1 hour. **3.** Add raisins in the cocoa-flavoured dough, red beans into the matcha-flavoured ones, and walnut into the milk-flavoured ones. **4.** Pour the dough into moulds, cut small crosses on the tops, and steam for 20 minutes and serve.

Variations

CORN CAKES – Use cornflour instead of plain flour and prepare as above.

YAM CAKES – Steam purples yaps, remove the skin and blend into a paste. Add the paste into plain flour and prepare as above.

奶香卷 (nai3 siang1 juan3)
MILKY ROLLS

These rolls are steamed to achieve an incredibly soft, sweet milky core.

Ingredients

•	flour	500g
•	baking powder	60g
•	yeast	75g
•	eggs	500g
•	butter	250g
•	milk	100g
•	sugar	500g
•	some water	

Preparation

1. Place broken eggs, melted butter, sugar and milk in a bowl, and mix thoroughly for later use. Add baking powder, yeast, water and flour, mix into dough, and break the dough into portions weighing about 25g each. Roll the portions into flat rectangles, brush the filling on, then roll up the dough and slice with a knife. 2. Let the rolls rise for 15 minutes at a temperature of 40°C, then steam for 10 minutes and serve.

Variations

CHOCO ROLLS – Mix cocoa powder, butter and sugar for the filling, and prepare as above.
MATCHA ROLLS – Mix matcha (green tea) powder, butter and sugar for the filling, and prepare as above.

富貴糕 (fu4 gui4 gao1)

PROSPERITY ROLLS

Prosperity Rolls are traditionally eaten at festivals. Combined with the slight sweetness of bean paste, this sweet and sticky roll is springy to the bite and truly delicious.

Ingredients

- glutinous flour   600g
- bean paste   400g
- sugar osmanthus   4tbsp
- some water

Preparation

1. Using 2 tablespoons of sugar osmanthus, water and glutinous flour, make a dough. Roll the dough into long sticks, then flatten the sticks, and roll into rectangles of 2mm in thickness and 8cm in width. Spread bean paste on the underside of the rectangles, roll up into cylinders, and cut the extra dough away. 2. Then, cut the rolls into portions of about 8cm long and place them into steamers. Steam on high heat for about 3 minutes and serve.

Variations

GREEN TEA PROSPERITY ROLLS – Add matcha (green tea) powder into the dough, and prepare as above.

SESAME PROSPERITY ROLLS – Crush sesame seeds into powder, and add sugar to make the filling.

BLACK SESAME PASTE PROSPERITY ROLLS – Use black sesame paste (a mixture of lard and sesame powder) as the filling.

MINTY PROSPERITY ROLLS – Cut and crush mint leaves, then add into the filling and prepare as above.

雙色蒸餃 (shuang1 se4 zheng1 jiao3)
DUOTONE DUMPLINGS

Duotone Dumplings are characterised by their vibrant colours, creative look and translucent skin. Filled with different ingredients, they give off different taste sensations.

Ingredients

•	fine white flour	250g	•	sesame oil	100g
•	glutinous flour	70g	•	sugar	10g
•	starch	70g	•	soy sauce	10g
•	pork thigh	200g	•	salt	10g
•	crab roe	200g	•	MSG	10g
•	frozen soup	500g	•	juice from shallots	10g
•	shepherd's purse vegetable	300g	•	juice from ginger	10g
•	cooking oil	50g			

Preparation

1. Dice the pork. Mix in frozen soup, salt, MSG, soy sauce, and sugar. Add the juices from ginger and shallot and mix, then mix in the cooking oil and sesame oil. After that, crush the frozen soup and mix into the meat to make the filling. 2. For the second filling, blanch the shepherd's purse till it's cooked, then dice it, and add salt, MSG and sugar. 3. Mix the fine white flour, starch, glutinous flour and sugar, and make a hole in the middle. Add in 9 parts hot water, and stir till the flour resembles snowflakes floating on the water. When it has cooled slightly, add in cold water and knead till it becomes dough. 4. Roll the dough into long sticks, and break it with your hand into 40 portions, then roll the portions into flat circles. 5. Shape the circles into 2 adjoining cups, then add in the 2 kinds of filling. Steam on high heat and serve.

Variations

"FOUR TASTES" DUMPLINGS – Make 4 kinds of filling by washing and crushing carrots, mushrooms, red chilli and peas, then adding condiments. Shape the dough into 4 adjoining cups and put the 4 kinds of filling into them respectively.

COUPLE DUMPLINGS – Mix carrot juice and spinach juice into 2 batches of dough to give it colour, then shape the 2 colours of dough into 2 adjoining cups. The rest of the preparations are as above.

翡翠蝦餃 (fei3 cui4 sia1 jiao3)
JADEITE PRAWN DUMPLINGS

Jadeite Prawn Dumplings are very popular in restaurants throughout Hong Kong and Taiwan. They don a rich green colour with the tail of a prawn peeking out of each dumpling.

Ingredients

• flour	450g	• salt	5g
• starch	50g	• MSG	5g
• prawns	500g	• sugar	5g
• spinach	300g	• sesame oil	5g
• fatty pork	125g	• pepper	5g
• dried bamboo shoots	125g		
• lard	90g		

Preparation

1. Wash and cut the fresh spinach into sections. Boil some water in a pot, blanch the spinach lightly, then turn off the fire and let it cool. Pour the spinach and water into a blender, blend, sieve and set aside. 2. Mix the spinach juice, flour, starch and salt, mix and add warm water. When evenly mixed, add lard and knead into balls of dough for later use. 3. Remove the heads and shells of the prawns, leaving only the tails, and drain of moisture. Dice the pork and bamboo shoots, then add some salt, sugar, MSG, sesame oil and pepper. Blend well. 4. Break off parts of the dough and flatten into dumpling skins, wrap in the pork filling, then place the prawns in and mould into dumplings. 5. Steam on high heat and serve.

Variations

DUCK WRAPPED IN BLACK RICE – Dice and slightly marinate duck meat. Take 350g of flour, 100g black rice flour, starch and salt and mix well. Add water and knead into dough. Roll into skins, wrap the duck in and steam till done.

鮮蝦餃 (xian1 xia1 jiao3)

FRESH PRAWN DUMPLINGS

Its thin skin and juicy filling is one of the most common traits of Cantonese dim sum.
Just one bite into one of these will leave you savouring the taste for days after.

Ingredients

- flour   500g
- lard   20g
- fine salt   25g
- boiling water   750g
- raw prawn flesh   500g
- fatty pork   150g
- MSG   10g
- sugar   15g
- sesame oil   5g
- pepper   1.5g

Preparation

1. Blend the flour with the boiling water and leave for 15 minutes. Then add in 20g of lard and work in evenly throughout, making the dough glisten. Roll the dough into long sticks, separate into portions weighing about 10g each, then press the portions into flat circles for the skin. **2.** Dice the prawns to make a paste. Cut the bamboo shoots into thin strips, soak in boiling water and press the water out. Cut the pork into thin strips and steam till done, and when it has cooled down, dice it. Place the shrimp paste in a bowl, add MSG and salt. Stir the paste, slamming it down occasionally, till it becomes springy. Then add in the bamboo shoots, pork, sugar, pepper, sesame oil and lard, and blend all of them to make the filling. **3.** Wrap into the skin, place into a steamer brushed with oil, and steam on high heat for 5 minutes.

Variations

"THREE TASTES" DUMPLINGS – Prepare as above. For the filling, blend starched prawn, diced chicken and prawns.

豆沙包 (dou4 sha1 bao1)
BEAN PASTE BUNS

A popular Chinese steamed dim sum dish that it is easy to make.

Ingredients

- flour   500g
- yeast   50g
- bean paste filling   250g
- some edible soda

Preparation

1. Place the flour in a large bowl. Add in some yeast that has been dissolved in warm water, add water, knead into dough and leave it to ferment. After it has risen, add in the soda and mix. Knead the risen dough into cylinders, break into portions and hand-flatten the portions. 2. Wrap the bean paste filling in and steam for 20 minutes on high heat.

Variations
BLACK SESAME PASTE BUNS – Prepare as above, but use black sesame paste (powdered sesame mixed with lard) for the filling.

玉米麵小窩頭 (yu4 mi3 mian4 xiao3 wo1 tou2)
SMALL CORNFLOUR BUNS

Small Cornflour Buns used to be the staple dish for the northern Chinese people. It has a rich and strong fragrance and at the same time, sweet and sticky to the taste.

Ingredients
- cornflour   500g
- glutinous flour   50g
- sugar   50g
- some warm water

Preparation
1. Mix the cornflour, glutinous flour and sugar into a smooth dough using warm water. 2. Separate into portions, hand-shape them into small "nests", and simply steam till done.

双色糕 (shuang1 se4 gao1)

DUOTONE RICE CAKES

Duotone Rice Cakes are colourful and sweet, soft and refreshing.

Ingredients

* purple glutinous rice   400g
* yellow glutinous rice   400g
* cooked flour   100g
* fine white sugar   300g

Preparation

1. Wash the two types of rice, put in a plate and steam till cooked. Using a clean wet cloth, crush the rice into a paste, while adding the sugar into the mix from time to time. 2. After the crushed rice has cooled, separate the rice in portions weighing about 50g each. Sprinkle the cooked flour on the rice cakes, put into the moulds. When the rice cakes are moulded, remove from the moulds and serve.

PAN-FRIED
DIM SUM

咸薄鐺 (xian2 bao2 cheng1)
SAVOURY PAN

The "pan", as the name implies, this dish is named for refers to a shallow saucepan. This is a speciality pan-fried Cantonese snack that has a thin and crispy skin, a varied and tender filling, and a delightful fragrance.

Ingredients

- dried shrimp   50g
- spring onion   3g
- egg   1
- Chinese sausage   100g
- flour   300g

- corn starch   100g
- glutinous rice flour 100g
- water   200g
- pepper   5g
- oil   100g

Preparation

1. Soak the shrimps in 100g warm water until it softens, dice, and keep the water for later use. Dice the sausage, stir-fry with the shrimps till fragrant, and set aside. Dice the spring onion, mix with the sausage and shrimps and you have the filling. 2. Mix the flour, corn starch, glutinous rice flour and a beaten egg, mix in the salt and pepper and pour in the 100g of water that was previously used to soak the shrimps in and pour in the rest of the water to make a paste. 3. Add a little oil to the saucepan, wait till it's 40% to boiling, then pour in a thin layer of paste. Lay the filling on carefully, and continue to pour in more paste. When the paste at the bottom has turned golden-brown, flip the pastry over. Remove when the other side has also turned golden-brown, slice and serve.

Variations

SWEET PAN – Simply substitute the shrimp, sausage, salt and pepper with crushed peanuts, white sesame, shredded coconut and sugar. Wrap into rectangular-based dumplings and steam.

香煎芋泥餅 (xiang1 jian1 yu2 ni2 bing3)
FRAGRANT YAM CRACKERS

These light green crackers are covered with fragrant sesame and filled with a pastel purple, slightly sweet yam filling. The multiple layers of flavours – sesame, green tea and yam – blend with each other seamlessly.

Ingredients

• glutinous rice flour	150g	• sesame	30g
• malt sugar	20g	• granulated sugar	10g
• water	50g	• butter	20g
• yam	300g	• vegetable oil	100g
• green tea powder	5g		

Preparation

1. Steam the yam till it is cooked. Skin and mash the yam. Heat butter in a wok and stir-fry the yam paste with sugar till dry, set aside and prepare the skin. Mix the glutinous rice flour, water and green tea powder, and knead into dough. 2. Separate the dough into 15 portions and wrap the yam filling into each dough. Roll in sprinkle. Pan-fry in oil till done.

Variations
PROSPERITY GREEN TEA CRACKERS
 – Simply substitute yam with red bean paste for the filling.
FRAGRANT PUMPKIN CRACKERS
 – Steam the pumpkin. Skin and mash the pumpkin. Squeeze out some moisture. Mix with glutinous rice flour, knead into dough, and wrap in red bean paste filling. Pan-fry in oil till done.

鳳尾蝦煎餃 (feng4 wei3 xia1 jian1 jiao3)
PHOENIX-TAIL PRAWN DUMPLING

The "phoenix tail", or the prawn's tail curls out of the dumpling, tempting the diner's eyes. This dumpling has a thin pan-fried base, packed with fresh and succulent prawns.

Ingredients

• dumpling skin	350g
• pond-bred prawns	20
• oyster sauce	5g
• salt	3g
• chicken essence	2g
• yellow wine	5g
• pepper	2g
• sugar	5g
• sesame oil	50g
• vegetable oil	5g
• water	100g

Preparation

1. Peel the prawns, leaving the ends of the prawns untouched. Wash and drain. Marinate with oyster sauce, salt, chicken essence, yellow wine, pepper, sugar and sesame oil for 15 minutes. Wrap a prawn into each dumpling skin, pressing the dumpling tight in the middle. Leave the ends open with a prawn tail curling out. 2. Heat a round saucepan. Spread out 30g oil and spread on the saucepan and place the dumpling firmly in. Pour in another 10g of oil and 100g of water, and cover the saucepan. Remove the cover 7 minutes later and pour in the remaining oil. Leave for a moment more. Serve with vinegar if desired.

Variations
"THREE TASTES" DUMPLINGS
– Dice pork, sea cucumbers and prawn. Mix with soy sauce, fine salt, cooking wine, diced spring onion and diced ginger, and use this for the filling.

CABBAGE PORK DUMPLINGS
– Dice cabbage. Squeeze in gauze to remove excess moisture. Mix with diced pork, soy sauce, salt, cooking wine and pepper. With the dumpling skin, wrap the filling into the shape of the common dumpling and pan-fry as above.

香煎蘿蔔糕 (xiang1 jian1 luo2 bo gao1)

PAN-FRIED CARROT CAKE

Pan-Fried Carrot Cake is a typical Cantonese snack, crispy on the outside and soft on the inside. The carrot and ham flavours make a perfect blend and tastes best when eaten hot.

Ingredients

- rice flour   400g
- turnip   200g
- cured meat   30g
- (about 2) Chinese mushrooms   10g
- salt   3g
- chicken essence   5g
- pepper   3g
- soy sauce   5g
- sesame oil   5g
- vegetable oil   50g

Preparation

1. Wash and dice the mushrooms and the meat. Wash and skin the turnips. Grate them into thin sticks, blanch and set aside. Add water to the flour to make a paste. Mix in the turnips, mushrooms and meat. Stir in salt, chicken essence, pepper, soy sauce and sesame oil. 2. Pour the paste into a square container and steam on high heat for 25 minutes. Remove when the paste has solidified, and cut into thick slices. Pour oil into a saucepan, and pan-fry till both sides are golden-brown. Serve with chilli sauce if desired.

香麻蝦餅 (xiang1 ma2 xia1 bing3)
SESAME PRAWN CRACKERS

Sesame Prawn Crackers are hard and full of sesame fragrance on the surface, but soft and chewy on the inside. The savoury meat and sweet corn blend together to form a unique flavour.

Ingredients

•	shelled prawn	400g	• sesame oil	2g
•	egg	3	• MSG	3g
•	fatty pork	50g	• salt	3g
•	sweet corn kernels	20g	• light soy sauce	10g
•	spring onion	3g	• pepper	3g
•	sesame	50g	• vegetable oil	100g

Preparation

1. Separate the egg whites and set aside. Dice the prawn and pork together to make a paste. Mix with egg whites, diced spring onion, MSG, salt, light soy sauce, pepper and corn. Stir in one direction till it becomes springy. Shape the paste into meatballs and flatten into circles about 1.5cm thick and 10cm across. Sprinkle with sesame. 2. Add a little oil to the saucepan. When the oil is 40% to boiling, pan-fry the raw crackers on medium heat. Remove when both sides are golden-brown. Drain the excess oil, slice and serve.

Variations
PRAWN CRACKERS
– Prepare as above, without the sesame. Skin and crush shepherd's purse to replace corn.

豬肉韭菜鍋貼 (zhu1 rou4 jiu3 cai4 guo1 tie1)

PAN-FRIED DUMPLINGS WITH PORK AND CHIVES

These dumplings have a smooth skin and a crispy fried base. Soup squirts out into your mouth with one bite, and the filling is savoury and succulent.

Ingredients

•	flour	500g	• ginger	50g
•	pork	350g	• cooking wine	20g
	(with 30% fat and 70% lean meat)		• soy sauce	35g
•	chives	100g	• salt	10g
•	sesame oil	50g	• pepper	10g
•	spring onion	50g	• vegetable oil	150g

Preparation

1. Mix 100g flour with cold water to make dough. Blanch the other 400g of flour till done. Mix with the cold dough and knead while the flour is still hot. Cover with a wet cloth and let it stand. 2. Dice the pork into a paste. Dice the chives, spring onion and ginger. Mix all these ingredients with 50g sesame oil, cooking wine, soy sauce, salt and pepper to make the filling. Roll the dough into long sticks. Snap off 50 small portions and roll into circular skins of about 8cm in diameter. Wrap the filling in, and shape like new moons. 3. Add some oil to a heated saucepan, and lay the dumplings in facing up. Add a little water, cover the saucepan, and pan-fry on medium heat. Remove and serve when the bases are golden-brown and the water has dried up.

Variations

PAN-FRIED DUMPLINGS WITH BEEF

– Substitute pork and chives with beef for the filling.

VEGETARIAN PAN-FRIED DUMPLINGS

– Make the skin as above. Dice bamboo shoots, dried tofu and mushrooms, and stir-fry. Add soy sauce, sugar and water, bring to a boil. Thicken with wet starch, add sesame oil and MSG. Blanch and dice shepherd's purse, add to the above mixture. Prepare as above.

PAN-FRIED DUMPLINGS WITH MUTTON

– Dice cabbage and squeeze out the excess moisture. Substitute pork and chives with mutton, onion and cabbage for the filling.

咖喱牛肉煎包 (ga1 li2 niu2 rou4 jian1 bao1)
PAN-FRIED CURRY BEEF BUNS

Pan-Fried Curry Beef Buns have a crispy, golden-brown pan-fried base and a snowy-white, light and soft skin. The filling is slightly spicy, but wonderfully succulent. The buns are very substantial in size, making it a satisfying light meal.

Ingredients

•	wheat flour	600g	• sugar	5g
•	beef	300g	• pepper	3g
•	curry powder	5g	• sesame oil	10g
•	onion	100g	• yeast	20g
•	cooking wine	5g	• vegetable oil	60g
•	salt	5g	• baking soda	2g
•	chicken essence	3g		

Preparation

1. Pour the flour into a basin. Add yeast and water. Knead into a hard dough and leave to stand. After the dough has risen, add the baking soda and roll into long sticks. Snap off 12 equally-sized portions, and roll into circular skins. 2. Peel the onion, wash and cut into thin strips. Blanch the onions. Dice the beef finely. Mix with sesame oil, onion, curry powder, cooking wine, salt, chicken essence, sugar and pepper, to get the filling. Wrap into the skin. Wrap into buns with folds on top. 3. Brush on oil in a heated saucepan and place the buns in facing up. Pour in cool water and cover the pan. Fry the buns and constantly turn the pan to make sure the heat is evenly distributed. After 10 minutes, the buns will turn golden-brown, and the skin will puff up. Fry the other side till golden-brown, and serve.

Variations

PAN-FRIED BEEF BUNS
– Use finely diced beef, diced spring onion, diced ginger, salt, sesame oil and MSG for the filling.

PAN-FRIED STRAW MUSHROOM BUNS
– Use diced pork, diced straw mushrooms, diced canola hearts, diced fresh bamboo shoots, peeled prawns, soy sauce, lard, diced spring onion, diced ginger, sesame oil and MSG for the filling.

PAN-FRIED PORK BUNS
– Use diced pork, diced dried mushrooms, lard, diced spring onion, diced ginger, salt, sesame oil and MSG for the filling.

韭菜香腸攤餅 (jiu3 cai4 xiang1 chang2 tan1 bing3)
CREPES WITH CHIVES AND SAUSAGE

These crepes are colourful and appealing and has a chewy and filling dough.

Ingredients

- sausage   40g
- chives   40g
- flour   100g
- egg   1
- water   20g
- vegetable oil   100g
- salt   5g

Preparation

1. Dice the sausage. Wash and dice the chives. Beat the egg. Pour flour into the egg and stir into a paste. Stir in 20g of water. Add the sausage, chives and salt. Mix well. 2. Add oil into a saucepan, and pour the dough in slowly. Using a spoon, spread the dough into an even layer of 2cm thickness. Cover the pan and fry on low heat. When one side is golden-brown, flip the dough and cover again. Remove when the other side turns golden-brown. Slice and serve.

臺式粟米餃 (tai2 shi4 su4 mi3 jiao3)
TAIWAN CORN DUMPLINGS

Corn Dumplings are small and delicate. You can see the golden-brown corn kernels through the thin skin and the liquids from the meat and corn squirt out all at once when you take a bite, filling your mouth with a delicious mix of the sweet and the savoury.

Ingredients

• dumpling skin	350g	• ginger	3g
• corn kernels	100g	• chicken essence	3g
• pork	100g	• vegetable oil	50g
• salt	5g	• water	100g
• cooking wine	10g		

Preparation

1. Dice the ginger and pork. Mix them with corn kernels. Add in salt and cooking wine for the filling. Wrap into the skins, closing only the middle and leaving the ends open. 2. Heat a saucepan and add 30g oil evenly. Lay the dumplings in facing up. Add 10g oil and 100g water. Cover the saucepan. Open up 7 minutes later, pour on the remaining oil, and leave for a moment more.

Variations
PAN-FRIED DUMPLINGS WITH CHIVES
– Use prawns, pork and diced chives with seasonings for the filling.

PAN-FRIED DUMPLINGS WITH PORK
– Use pork (with 30% fat and 70% lean meat), salt, spring onion, ginger, cooking wine and MSG for the filling.

鲜肉生煎 (xian1 rou4 sheng1 jian1)

PAN-FRIED PORK BUNS

Pan-Fried Buns are a well-known Shanghai snack. The base is crispy and fragrant, the skin light and puffy. The real essence of the bun, however, is the abundance of soup inside.

Ingredients

- flour   500g
- fresh yeast   15g
- fatty pork   500g
- frozen lard gelatin   200g
- peanut oil   100g
- sesame oil   25g
- spring onion   25g
- cooking wine   15g
- soft white sugar 20g
- MSG   1g
- sesame   25g
- ginger   10g

Preparation

1. Dice the spring onion, ginger and pork. Mix pork, soy sauce, MSG, cooking wine, soft white sugar, ginger and 15g spring onion, and leave for a while. Pour in water, add gelatin and sesame oil, and stir till springy to get the filling. 2. Pour flour into a basin. Add 200g boiling water and stir continously so the flour resembles snowflakes on the water. Dissolve yeast in warm water, make into a paste, and add to the flour. Add 15g warm water, stir and knead. Cover with cloth and leave for an hour, then knead again. Roll the dough into long sticks, snap off small portions weighing 15g each, and flatten. Wrap 150g into each skin and close the openings. 3. Heat a saucepan and add 30g oil. Lay the dumplings in facing up. Add some oil and cover the saucepan. Open up 2 minutes later and pour 150g cold water into the sides. Cover and leave for 5 to 6 minutes more. Turn the pan now and again to make sure the heat is evenly distributed. When the pan emits fragrance and a lot of steam, remove the lid and sprinkle on the remaining spring onions and sesame. Remove when the dumpling bases are golden-brown. Serve hot.

菜肉煎餅 (cai4 rou4 jian1 bing3)
PIES WITH VEGETABLE AND PORK

This dish is a new take on a traditional Chinese dish. The skin is soft and smooth, and the filling savoury and succulent, especially when dipped in vinegar.

Ingredients

• wheat flour	500g
• fatty pork	150g
• chives	200g
• fresh bamboo shoots	100g
• salt	8g
• MSG	2g
• cooking wine	15g
• vegetable oil	50g

Preparation

1. Wash and dice the chives. Wash and slice the bamboo shoots. Dice the pork finely. Put all of them into a basin and stir in one direction till springy. Add salt, MSG, cooking wine and mix all the ingredients for the filling. 2. Add warm water to the flour and knead well. Roll the dough into long sticks and snap off 20 equally-sized portions weighing 15g each. Roll into skins, wrap in the filling, and flatten slightly. 3. Heat a saucepan and add 30g oil. Lay the dumplings in facing up. Add the remaining oil and fry on medium heat till one side is golden-brown. Flip and fry till both sides are golden-brown. Remove and serve with vinegar.

Variations

PRAWN PIES – Use mixed prawns and pork for the filling.
PIES WITH CABBAGE AND PORK – Dice cabbage and squeeze in gauze to remove excess moisture. Mix with diced pork for the filling.

菌菇煎包 (jun1 gu1 jian1 bao1)
PAN-FRIED MUSHROOM BUNS

Pan-Fried Mushroom Buns are a well-known traditional snack that originated from the Heze area in Shandong province. They feature a crispy, golden-brown base, a snowy-white, light and soft skin, and a succulent mushroom filling.

Ingredients

• wheat flour	600g
• mushrooms	120g
• fatty pork	120g
• yeast	20g
• bamboo shoots	60g
• spring onion	10g
• ginger	10g
• salt	5g
• MSG	3g
• soy sauce	6g
• sesame oil	100g
• lard	120g

Preparation

1. Dice the spring onion and ginger. Wash, blanch and cool the mushrooms with water. Drain and dice the mushrooms. Remove the coverings and hard parts of the bamboo shoots. Wash and dice the bamboo shoots. Dice the pork finely and mix with mushrooms and bamboo shoots. Add ginger, salt, MSG, soy sauce, sesame oil and 50g lard for the filling. 2. Add warm water to the flour and knead well. Roll the dough into long sticks, snap off 20 equally-sized portions weighing 15g each. Roll into skins, wrap in the filling, and close the openings. 3. Heat a saucepan and add 50g lard. Lay the dumplings in facing up. Add the remaining lard and cover. Open up the lid 2 minutes later and pour 150g cold water in. Cover and leave for 5 to 6 minutes more. Turn the pan now and again to make sure the heat is evenly distributed. When the pan emits fragrance and a lot of steam, remove the lid and sprinkle on the spring onion. Remove when the dumpling bases are golden-brown.

Variations
PAN-FRIED BEEF BUNS
– Use beef for the filling.
PAN-FRIED TAI'AN BUNS
– Use pork, chives and cooked vermicelli for the filling.

煎班戟 (jian1 ban1 ji3)

FRIED PANCAKES

Fried Pancakes used to be a Hong Kong-style dessert adapted from Western pancakes. They gradually evolved into a savoury snack of paper-thin pancakes with a sweet and savoury filling.

Ingredients

• flour	100g	• spring onion	3g
• salt	10g	• ginger	2g
• egg	1	• soy sauce	20g
• fresh milk	250ml	• cooking wine	10g
• soft white sugar	10g	• starch	200g
• pork	100g	• vegetable oil	50g

Preparation

1. Mix flour with 3g salt in a basin. Add a beaten egg and pour in half the milk slowly while stirring. Beat until the paste is smooth and add the remaining milk to get the pancake dough.
2. Dice the pork, spring onion and ginger. Mix with 7g salt, sugar, soy sauce, cooking wine and starch. Stir in one direction till springy, and stir-fry in oil to make the filling. 3. Pour a little oil into a saucepan, heat, and rotate the saucepan to spread the oil evenly. Pour away any excess oil. Pour in the pancake dough when the oil is 80% to boiling and rotate the saucepan to spread the dough evenly. When it has solidified slightly, add the filling. Fold up the pancake, first from left to right, then from top to bottom. The pancake will form a rectangle with the filling in. Continue frying on medium heat till the pancake turns golden-brown. Constantly flip the pancake to fry evenly.

Variations

FRIED PANCAKES WITH FRUITS, RED BEANS AND STICKY RICE CAKE

– Slice bananas diagonally. Slice sticky rice cakes. Add red bean paste to the above, and use for the filling. Before serving the pancakes, sprinkle with icing sugar.

FRIED PANCAKES WITH CHRYSANTHEMUM

– Fry pancakes and remove when they solidify. Mix wild chrysanthemums, corn starch and granulated sugar with water and wrap the mixture into the pancakes.

香酥油餅 (xiang1 su1 you2 bing3)
FRAGRANT FRIED PANCAKES

Fragrant Fried Pancakes are extremely easy to prepare. Made with simple ingredients, these delicious fried pancakes are crispy on the outside and soft on the inside with a strong spring onion fragrance.

Ingredients

• flour	500g
• fresh yeast	15g
• spring onion	10g
• white sesame	5g
• salt	10g
• vegetable oil	50g

Preparation

1. Dice the spring onion. 2. Pour flour into a basin. Add 200g boiling water and stir until the flour becomes like snowflakes on the water. Dissolve yeast in warm water. Make into a paste and add to the flour. Add 15g warm water, spring onions, salt, and stir. Cover with cloth and leave for an hour, then knead again. Roll the dough into a pancake about as thick as a finger. Sprinkle sesame on both sides. 3. Heat a saucepan and add oil. Pan-fry the pancake on medium heat. When one side turns golden-brown, flip and fry till the other side turns the same colour. Remove, cut into small pieces and serve.

臺式韭菜蝦皮茄子煎 (tai2 shi4 jiu3 cai4 xia1 pi2 qie2 zi jian1)
TAIWANESE EGGPLANTS WITH CHIVES AND PRAWNS

This dish is rather sophisticated and uncommon in other areas of China. It is crispy on the outside and soft on the inside and contains many nutrients and minerals like vitamin C and calcium. In traditional Chinese medicine, eggplants can also help to remove excess 'yang' energy, or heatiness that causes sore throat and fever, from the body.

Ingredients

- eggplants   350g
  (also known as brinjals or aubergines)
- chives   150g
- prawn shells   45g
- egg   1
- flour   200g
- salt   8g
- pepper   3g
- chicken essence   3g
- cooking wine   10g
- vegetable oil   100g

Preparation

1. Chop the eggplants into 5cm-long sections. Slice every section lengthwise into 3 pieces. Steam till done and let cool. Wash and dice the chives. Wash and drain the prawn shells. Beat the egg. Marinate the eggplants and prawn shells with 10g oil, salt, pepper, chicken essence and cooking wine for 5 minutes. Stir in the flour and egg. 2. Heat oil in a saucepan and pour the mixture in a circle. Pan-fry till you see bubbles. Flip and pan-fry till both sides are dark yellow. Remove, drain and serve.

南瓜餅 (nan2 gua1 bing3)
PUMPKIN CRACKERS

Pumpkin Crackers are soft, sticky and sweet without being too cloying. The fragrance of pumpkin and sesame are simply irresistible.

Ingredients

• pumpkin	300g
• granulated sugar	50g
• glutinous rice flour	200g
• round crackers	200g
• vegetable oil	140g
• white sesame	50g

Preparation

1. Skin, seed and steam the pumpkin till done. Mash and mix in sugar and glutinous rice flour while the pumpkin is still hot. Rub into small balls. Take 2 crackers and sandwich a ball in between. Flatten and sprinkle a circle of sesame around the exposed pumpkin. 2. Pan-fry thoroughly on low heat, remove, drain and serve.

Variations

YAM CRACKERS – Prepare as above, substituting pumpkin with yam.

炸点

DEEP-FRIED
DIM SUM

香炸奶黃包 (xiang1 zha4 nai3 huang2 bao1)
FRIED CUSTARD BUNS

Sink your teeth through the thin and crispy skins of these buns and savour
the soft, creamy and delicate custard filling.

Ingredients

• all-purpose flour	250g	• non-glutinous flour	34g
• yeast powder	8g	• cheese powder	20g
• baking soda	4g	• milk powder	20g
• sugar	5g	• water	90ml
• warm water	125ml	• sugar	100g
• eggs	2	• butter	35g

Preparation

1. Melt the yeast powder in warm water. Mix flour and 5g sugar into the yeast solution bit by bit, stirring with chopsticks as you go. Knead the mixture into a smooth and shiny dough. Place the dough in a large covered bowl and let it ferment for an hour till it doubles in size. To test, stick a chopstick in. If the dough does not bounce back, fermentation is complete. Knead for another 10 minutes to expel the air. Separate the dough into 50g portions, and roll into flat circles. 2. Beat the butter. Add the 100ml of sugar in 2 portions, and continue to beat. Add in the eggs, beaten, in 3 portions, stir, and pour in the 90ml of water. Mix non-glutinous flour, cheese powder and milk powder. Pour into the same mixture and stir to form a paste. Pour some warm water into a pot, put it on low heat. Steam the paste above water and stir constantly till it achieves the consistency of mud. 3. Wrap the filling into the dough, steam till done, and deep-fry till golden-brown.

Variations
CREAMY "QUICKSAND" CUSTARD BUNS
– Prepare the ingredients as above. Steam a
salted egg, discard the egg white, crush the yolk
into pieces, and mix with soft white sugar and
cream for the filling.

起酥麻花(qi3 su1 ma1 hua1)
FRIED CHEESE BRAIDS

Compared to ordinary fried braids known as "Ma Hua", these easy-to-make, delicious treats are even crispier and easier to bite into.

Ingredients
- cheese   3
- soft sugar   200g
- cooking oil   600g

Preparation
1. Cut every piece of cheese lengthwise into 9 strips, then roll each one into a tight cylinder. Tie 3 cylinders together like a hair-braid. 2. Heat the oil in a wok to about 180°C, put in the braids and deep-fry till they become golden-brown. Remove, drain and coat in soft sugar. Serve.

Variations
SANZI FRIED BRAIDS – see pg116
CRISPY FRIED BRAIDS – Knead flour, brown sugar, baking soda and vegetable oil into dough. Leave it for a while and roll into long sticks. Brush some oil on and leave it to stand again. After a while, roll into longer sticks and leave to stand again for 30 minutes. Roll them even longer for the third time, and fold 1 stick into 3. Heat oil till it is about 30% to boiling, then deep-fry till done.

FRIED BRAIDS WITH WINE LEES
– The preparation is much like Crispy Fried Braids, with some wine lees and lard added to the dough before kneading.
TIANJIN FRIED BRAIDS – see pg116

千層蘿蔔絲 (qian1 ceng2 luo2 bo si1)

TURNIP LAYERS

A must-have in any Cantonese cuisine, Turnip Layers is a crispy yet soft and fragrant dim sum dish.

Ingredients

• high-gluten flour	340g	• yeast	4g
• low-gluten flour	35g	• turnip	300g
• milk	130g	• pork	150g
• margarine	250g	• ham	20g
• eggs	3	• essence of chicken	5g
• soft white sugar	50g	• sesame oil	2g
• salt	4g	• white lard	10g

Preparation

1. Melt the margarine at room temperature. Using a rolling pin, press the margarine into a flat rectangle. 2. Beat 2 eggs into the 2 types of flour. Mix the yeast with warm milk, then pour in the flour bit by bit. Knead into dough. Wrap in cling wrap and leave to ferment for 30 minutes. Roll the dough into a rectangle about 3 times the size of the margarine. Place the margarine in the middle, and wrap it up in the dough. Flip the dough over, and using a rolling pin, beat it lightly till it becomes bigger. Flip it over again, and roll into a rectangle. Fold the two sides towards the middle, then fold it in half. Cover with cling wrap and leave to stand for 20 minutes. Remove the cling wrap. Once again, roll into a rectangle, fold the two sides towards the middle, fold it in half, cover with cling wrap and leave to stand for 20 minutes. Repeat the whole procedure once more and remove the cling wrap. Using a rolling pin, roll the dough till it is bigger and about 0.7cm thick. Cut into 4 long strips, each about 5cm wide. 3. Beat 1 egg and stack the 4 strips together, with egg between each strip. Afterwards, cut vertically into thin layers each about 0.5cm thick, roll the layers till they are thin, and cut into small rectangles. 4. Dice the turnip and ham, and dice the pork finely. Stir-fry all of them with the white lard, essence of chicken, sesame oil and salt to make the filling. Wrap the filling into the dough, hand-shape them into the desired shape, then deep-fry and serve.

Variations

DURIAN PUFFS – Make the skin as above, and use durian flesh as the filling.

LOTUS PASTE PUFFS – Make the skin as above, and use lotus paste as the filling.

PAPAYA PUFFS – Make the skin as above. To make the filling, cook, skin and seed a papaya, and mash the flesh.

PUMPKIN PUFFS – Make the skin as above. Skin a ripe pumpkin and steam till done, then add peanut powder, sesame powder, honeyed dates and sugar to make the filling.

TURNIP PUFFS – see pg117

綠豆酥餅 (lü3 dou4 su1 bing3)
GREEN BEAN PUFFS

The lingering fragrance of the green beans makes this light,
refreshing snack perfect for a tea-time treat.

Ingredients

• syrup	200ml	• high-gluten flour	50g
• baking soda	5g	• green beans	300g
• water	5g	• lard	20g
• peanut oil	60ml	• sugar	50g
• low-gluten flour	250g		

Preparation

1. Mix the baking soda with water. Pour into the flour together with syrup and peanut oil. Knead into dough, cover with cling wrap and leave to stand for 30 minutes. Separate into small portions weighing about 30g each. 2. Wash the green beans and soak it overnight. Rub the skin off and wash again after soaking. Boil in water, noting that the volume of the water should be twice the volume of the beans. Remove any foam that comes up with boiling. Cook the beans on high heat till it becomes mushy. Sieve, then add sugar and lard, stew on low heat. Keep stirring the mixture, and cook till it becomes a lumpy paste. Let it cool, then rub into portions weighing about 30g each. 3. Wrap the filling in the dough, then roll the balls till they become round. Place into the moulds and press lightly. Pre-heat an oven to 220°C, then bake the puffs for 8 to 10 minutes. Remove, brush on some yolk and bake for another 10 minutes. Remove from the oven and moulds, then deep-fry on high heat till golden-brown.

Variations

BEAN PASTE PUFFS – Prepare as above. Substitute green beans with red beans, or use ready-made red bean paste.

DATE PASTE PUFFS – Prepare as above. Substitute the green date paste with red bean paste.

LOTUS PASTE PUFFS – Prepare as above. Substitute green bean paste with lotus paste.

油墩子 (you2 dun1 zi)
FRIED BLOCKS

These golden-brown snacks are commonly seen on the streets of Shanghai in autumn and winter. The irresistible combination of turnip and spring onions will have you craving for more.

Ingredients

• flour	2500g	• diced spring onions	50g
• yeast powder	10g	• peanut oil	5000g
• turnip	3500g	• water	1500g
• fine salt	100g	• cold water	2500g
• MSG	10g		

Preparation

1. Wash and drain the turnip. Grate into strips each about as thick as a matchstick stalk. Squeeze dry in a clean piece of gauze, and mix with the diced spring onions. 2. Add in the flour, fine salt and MSG in a large bowl. Pour in 2500g of cold water and mix. Then pour in 1500g of water in 4 to 5 portions, and stir in a constant direction. Leave to stand for 1 to 2 hours. Add in the yeast powder and knead into dough. 3. Heat the peanut oil on high heat till it is about 80% to 90% to boiling. Pre-heat your ladle in the oil, then remove and pour 25g of the mixed dough into the ladle. Put 20g of turnip onto the dough, then cover with another 40g of dough. Shake a little to ensure the turnip is completely covered. Deep-fry the dough while still in the ladle, tipping it out only when it has solidified on the outside. Repeat for the other blocks. 4. Remove the blocks when they turn golden-brown, drain and serve.

Variations

FRIED BLOCKS WITH PORK – Dice some fatty pork. Add salt, cooking wine, soy sauce, sesame oil, diced ginger, diced spring onions, MSG and a little water. Mix well. Add a little diced shepherd's purse into the dough, and deep-fry as above.

苔條麻花 (tai2 tiao2 ma2 hua1)
FRIED BRAIDS WITH SEAWEED

Deep-fried to a golden crisp, this popular beer snack lends the unique taste of
seaweed for an added appeal.

Ingredients

• flour	500g
• cooking oil	100g
• seaweed	50g
• sugar	100g
• salt	10g
• yeast powder	3g
• egg	1

Preparation

1. Heat the cooking oil. Pour in diced seaweed, deep-fry till crispy and crush. Dissolve 100g of
sugar, 10g of salt, 3g of yeast powder and the egg in water, then mix with flour and knead into
dough. Leave to stand for 30 minutes, and roll into cakes about as thick as fingers. Brush the cakes
with oil and cut into strips. 2. Rub the strips till they are about as thick as chopsticks. Using both
your hands, rub them in the opposite direction. Pick up the 2 ends and press them together, so that
they naturally form braids. Roll the braids tighter, and once again pick up the 2 ends and press
them together. Leave the braids to stand for 10 minutes. 3. Heat the cooking oil till it is about 40%
to 50% to boiling and place the braids in. Fry on low heat till the braids float to the surface and
turn colour. Remove, drain and cool.

Variations
OSMANTHUS FRIED BRAIDS – Prepare as
above, using osmanthus instead of the seaweed.
Remove salt from the recipe.

江米條 (jiang1 mi3 tiao2)
RICE STICKS

Crispy, refreshingly sweet and not too oily, this fuss-free favourite makes a perfect, home-made snack for lazy days.

Ingredients

- glutinous rice flour   200g
- flour   100g
- sugar   50g
- water   100ml
- yeast powder   2g

Preparation

1. Mix all the ingredients, knead into dough, cover with cling wrap and leave for 10 minutes. Roll into thin pieces about 2mm thick, cut into strips about 5cm long and rub into cylinders. 2. Heat the cooking oil till it is about 50% to 60% to boiling, place the strips in and deep-fry till golden-brown. Remove and serve with syrup, fine white sugar or honey.

南瓜餅 (nan2 gua1 bing3)

PUMPKIN CAKES

Pumpkin Cakes are a traditional home-made snack consumed during the Winter Solstice festival. These delicious cakes use pumpkin to lend a heavenly fragrance, and they are extremely easy to make.

Ingredients

•	glutinous rice flour	400g
•	pumpkin	250g
•	sugar	50g
•	vegetable oil	15g
•	red bean paste	180g

Preparation

1. Steam the pumpkin, remove the skin and mash. Knead the pumpkin, glutinous rice flour and sugar into dough. Steam the dough in a steamer till half-done. Remove and put into a large bowl brushed with oil. Let it cool, then knead thoroughly and divide into 12 portions. Wrap 15g of red bean paste into each portion. 2. Deep-fry each portion on medium heat till golden-brown, remove, drain and serve.

Variations

YAM CAKES – Prepare as above, and use yam instead of pumpkin.

SICHUAN PUMPKIN CAKES – Prepare as above but without any filling. After kneading the dough, make it into a flat circular cake, roll in bread crumbs, and deep-fry on medium heat.

糖衣果 (tang2 yi1 guo3)

SUGAR-COATED FRUITS

A specialty of Shanghi, this crispy, delightful treat is soft and snowy-white in its centre.

Ingredients

• glutinous rice flour	800g
• flour	200g
• fresh yeast	8g
• peanut oil	1500g
• sugar	500g
• soft white sugar	20g

Preparation

1. Mix the glutinous rice flour and flour. Dissolve the yeast in 500g of warm water. Pour into the flour mixture and knead into dough. Cover with cloth, and leave to ferment. After fermentation, rub into circular sticks about 5cm across, and cut into 10cm-long sections. Make the ends of the sticks round. 2. Heat the peanut oil till it is about 60% to boiling. Deep-fry the sticks till they are golden-brown. Remove, drain, coat with soft white sugar and serve.

粢飯糕 (ci1 fan4 gao1)

GLUTINOUS RICE CAKES

Crispy and slightly charred on the outside, soft and fragrant on the inside, these deep-fried rice cakes are a popular breakfast snack in the Jiangnan province of China.

Ingredients
- japanese rice   1000g
- peanut oil   500g
- salt   20g

Preparation

1. Wash the rice and pour into a pot. Add water till the water level is 5cm higher than the surface of the rice and add 20g salt in. Boil the water on high heat, then switch to low heat and remove the cover. Cook for another 10 minutes till all the rice has expanded, with only a bit of water left on the surface. Cover the pot and cook on low heat for another 10 minutes. 2. Brush oil onto a large square container and pour the rice in. Cover the rice with a clean wet cloth, press it flat firmly and remove the cloth. Let it cool, then cut into rectangular blocks as seen in the picture. 3. Boil oil in a wok and slide in the blocks from the side of the wok, stirring lightly as you do so. Remove when the blocks turn golden-brown.

炸響鈴 (zha4 xiang3 ling2)
FRIED "BELLS"

These deep-fried treats, with a resemblance of a horse's bell, have a lovely
golden-brown hue and a sweet fragrance of beans.

Ingredients
- tofu skin — 5 sheets
- lean pork — 50g
- egg yolk — 1/4g
- shaoxing cooking wine — 10g

Preparation
1. Cover the tofu skins with a wet cloth till they soften. Wash and dice the pork. Mix with salt, MSG, egg yolk and Shaoxing cooking wine. Divide into 5 portions. Cut the tofu skins into rectangles. Crush the leftover bits, except the hard bits at the side, for later use. 2. Place one portion of the filling on one end of the tofu skin. Spread into a strip about 1 inch wide. Sprinkle on the crushed tofu skin, and roll up. Seal the roll with water, and repeat for the other 4 rolls. Cut each roll into little rolls about 1 inch wide each, and place them upright. 3. Heat oil till it is about 50% to boiling. Deep-fry the "bells", stirring constantly. When they turn golden-brown, remove, drain and serve. Serve with sweet bean sauce and/or spicy salt (Sichuan peppercorns mixed with salt) if desired.

Variations
FRIED CHICKEN "BELLS" – Prepare as above, and use chicken instead of pork.
FRIED VEGETARIAN "BELLS" – Wash, skin and mash some Chinese yam. Mix in salt and MSG. Wash and steam carrots, winter bamboo shoots and pre-soaked dried mushrooms. Dice them and stir-fry, adding soy sauce, cooking wine and MSG. Mix all the above ingredients with some flour. Wrap the filling in tofu skin, cut into pieces and deep-fry.

炸素丸子 (zha4 su4 wan2 zi)

VEGETARIAN FRIED BALLS

Though deep-fried, the ingredients used in this recipe do not absorb oil readily, and hence makes for a wonderful snack for the health-conscious.

Ingredients

- carrots   150g
- fermented tofu   300g
- lotus stems   100g
- salt   3g
- MSG   2g
- ginger   2g
- starch   8g
- spicy salt   3g
  (Sichuan peppercorns mixed with salt)
- salad oil   200g

Preparation

1. Chop the tofu finely and place into a big bowl. Skin and wash the carrots and lotus stems, then cut into pieces about as big as peas. Wash and dice ginger. Add 1 part water to 1 part starch and mix. 2. Blanch the carrot and lotus stem pieces and let cool in a plate. Mix in the tofu, salt, MSG, ginger and starch. 3. Heat oil till it is about 70% to boiling. Grab some mixture with your hands and squeeze a ball out from between the bases of your index ginger and thumb. Deep-fry till crispy and light brown. Sprinkle on the spicy salt and serve.

炸香糕 (zha4 xiang1 gao1)
FRAGRANT FRIED CAKES
Chewy and savoury, these fried cakes emit an intense flavour guaranteed to impress.

Ingredients
- tofu skin noodles (houbaiye)   200g (4 large sheets)
- cinnamon skin   1
- tsaoko fruits   2
- pelargonium (rose geranium)   3
- cloves   3
- dried mandarin orange peel   1
- ginger   5g
- spring onions   3g
- brown rock sugar   25g
- cooking wine   10g
- light soy sauce   35g
- dark soy sauce   15g
- salt   12g
- peanut oil   200g

Preparation
1. Mix all the ingredients together to make a marinate. Stew on low heat for 2 hours, and soak the tofu skin noodles in overnight. Heat the soup again the next day and scoop out the hot tofu skin noodles. Stack and wrap them tightly in gauze, press them tight with force and leave aside. When they have cooled, cut into pieces and you have the cakes. Cut the cakes into small pieces, as seen in the picture. 2. Heat the peanut oil till boiling. Deep-fry the cakes till dark- brown, remove, drain and serve.

炸臭豆腐 (zha4 chou4 dou4 fu)

FRIED SMELLY TOFU

Smelly Tofu is a typical Chinese dish. Foul-smelling as it is, this deceiving dish is in fact fragrant and extremely tasty.

Ingredients
- smelly tofu   250g
- peanut oil   500g

Preparation
1. Cut the smelly tofu into little cubes, heat the oil till boiling, and deep-fry on high heat till they turn golden-brown. 2. Remove, drain and serve. To preserve the softness on the inside, take care to not deep-fry for too long.

Variations
SMELLY TOFU WITH VERMICELLI
 – see pg117
HUNAN FRIED SMELLY TOFU
 – Mix chilli oil, sesame oil and chicken soup into a sauce. Heat rapeseed oil till 80% to boiling. Deep-fry for 5 minutes, remove and drain. Poke a hole in the middle of each cube with a chopstick, and pour the sauce in.

蛋黃條 (dan4 huang2 tiao2)

YOLK STRIPS

This delightful, ultra-crispy snack makes a satisfying crackling noise when bitten into.

Ingredients

• eggs	3
• flour	200g
• yeast powder	5g
• sugar	100g
• malt sugar	10g
• water	200g
• vegetable oil	500g

Preparation

1. Separate the yolks from the whites. Mix the flour and yeast powder, then pour in the yolks. Knead till the dough is smooth and non-sticky. Cover with cling wrap and leave for 30 minutes. Then roll the dough into thin pieces, and cut into short and thin strips. Sprinkle on dry flour to prevent sticking. 2. Heat the oil to 160°C, place the strips in and fry thoroughly on high heat, stirring with chopsticks constantly till the strips become hard and golden-brown. Remove and set aside.
4. Boil the sugar in water on medium heat. Put in the malt sugar and stew on low heat till you get syrup. Pour the strips in and mix quickly. Pour into a square container brushed with oil and press tight with a ladle. As soon as it has cooled, remove from the mould and cut into pieces.

杏仁蝦肉小塘菜餅 (xing4 ren3 xia1 rou4 xiao3 tang2 cai4 bing3)
ALMOND SHRIMP VEGETABLE CAKES

Non-greasy and appetising, they are refreshing a snack that uses almond, squid and vegetables for a unique combination of textures and flavours.

Ingredients

- squid   300g
- fatty pork   20g
- egg   1
- corn starch   2g
- pepper   2g
- small green vegetables   50g
- roasted almond slices   30g
- salt   3g

Preparation

1. Separate the egg white and set aside. Tear off the thin layer of "skin" on the squid, wash and slice. Blend the squid, pork, egg white and pepper into a paste using a blender. Alternatively, you can use ready-made squid paste. 2. Wash and dice the vegetables. Mix into the paste and place in a square mould. Stick some almond slices in and carefully deep-fry in pre-heated oil. Slice and serve.

Variations

CRISPY VEGETABLES – Dice the vegetables.
Mix into dough and deep-fry.
Serve with salad dressing

蘇式炸糖年糕 (su1 shi4 zha4 tang2 nian2 gao1)
SUZHOU FRIED SWEET NEW YEAR CAKES

A must-have during Chinese New Year, these auspicious sweet cakes have a lightly crisp crust and a sticky, sweet centre with a faint floral hint.

Ingredients
- glutinous rice flour   5000g
- brown sugar   400g
- sugar   400g
- honey osmanthus   100g
- sesame oil   2500g

Preparation
1. Add water to 2000g of glutinous rice flour. Mix into a paste and put into boiling water. Cook on high heat. With another 1500g of glutinous rice flour, mix with 50g honey osmanthus, brown sugar and half of the cooked flour. Knead into a red lump of dough. Knead the remaining 1500g of glutinous rice flour with the rest of the ingredients into a white lump of dough. 2. Shape the 2 lumps into long sticks. Place them side-to-side and knead them together lightly. Cut into small pieces about 3cm wide. 3. Heat the sesame oil till it is about 60% to boiling. Put in the dough and fry till the white part becomes golden-brown. Remove, drain and serve.

SANZI FRIED BRAIDS
(San3 Zi Ma2 Hua1)

Preparations
Knead 1250g of flour, 20g baking soda, 150g brown sugar, 15g vegetable oil and some water into a dough. Roll the dough into long sticks, leave it for awhile, then break off little lumps weighing about 50g each. Roll the lumps into even thinner long sticks, and coat each one with sesame seeds. Take 2 sticks and fold the ends together twice, so that they become 8 sticks. Pull the sticks till they are about 25cm long, press the ends together till they are tapered. Heat oil till it is about 60% to boiling, and fry the sticks till they become golden-brown. See pg84.

TIANJIN FRIED BRAIDS
(Tian1 Jin1 Da4 Ma2 Hua1)

Preparations
Knead flour, yeast, caustic soda with water, and sugar water together into dough. Leave it for a while, then shape into flat strips. Cut into strips about 1cm wide. Break the strips into 2 types, one 36cm long and one 26cm long. Sprinkle the short ones with sesame, then roll them so they become 36cm long. These are the "sesame sticks". Dice unripe plums, sugared ginger and walnuts into powder. Mix them with flour, pea-

nut oil, sugar, osmanthus and caustic soda with water, and knead into dough. Shape the dough into sticks about 36cm long. These are the "filling sticks". Twist 1 "filling stick", 7 uncoated sticks, and 2 "sesame sticks" together, deep-fry and serve. See pg84.

TURNIP PUFFS
(Lo2 Bo Si1 Su1 Jiao3)

Preparations
Make the skin as above. Cut a turnip into strips, blanch and stir-fry in margarine and salt. Wrap the turnip into the skin, roll up and shape into a an oval that resembles that of a duck's egg. See pg87.

SMELLY TOFU WITH VERMICELLI
(Guo4 Qiao2 Chou4 Dou4 Fu)

Preparations
Cut the smelly tofu into cubes. Heat the oil till 50% to 60% to boiling. Deep-fry till golden-brown, remove and drain. Serve on fried crispy vermicelli, covered with sweet and spicy sauce. See pg108.

烙点

GRILLED
DIM SUM

鲜肉月餅 (xian1 rou4 yue4 bing3)

PORK MOONCAKES

Pork Mooncakes are unique to Shanghai and they taste completely different from their Cantonese counterparts. The skin is light and puffy and the filling is succulent and smooth. Stores famous for Pork Mooncakes usually spot a long queue, and you can always smell them from a mile away.

Ingredients

•	flour	1000g	• salt	15g
•	cooked lard	400g	• sugar	5g
•	malt sugar	100g	• spring onion juice	5g
•	lean pork	750g	• ginger juice	5g
•	cooking wine	10g	• MSG	3g

Preparation

1. Wash and dice the pork finely. Mix in cooking wine, salt, sugar, MSG, spring onion juice and ginger juice. Stir well in a single direction to make the filling. 2. Put 400g flour into a large bowl. Add 200g cooked lard and knead thoroughly to make the second skin. Take 600g flour and put in another bowl. Add 200g cooked lard, malt sugar and a little warm water and knead thoroughly to make the skin. Shape the skin dough into balls, flatten and wrap the second skin dough in, then shape into balls. Roll the dough into a rectangle and fold 3 times. Roll into a rectangle about 65cm long and 50cm wide. Roll up along its width. Shape into a long strip about 3.3cm wide. Cut into 30 portions and flatten each one. Wrap the filling in each and close the opening. Roll into a ball then flatten slightly. These are the raw mooncakes. 3. Brush a layer of oil in a saucepan and lay the mooncakes neatly in. Grill on low heat till both sides are light-yellow and serve.

Variations

MOONCAKES WITH LARD AND BEAN PASTE – Substitute pork with red bean paste and lard for the filling.

MOONCAKES WITH HAM AND LARD – Mix diced ham, lard and sugar for the filling.

香菇豬肉餡餅 (xiang1 gu1 zhu1 rou4 xian4 bing3)
MUSHROOM PORK PIES

These golden-brown pies are ideal for the masses. They are easy to make and have a juicy and savoury filling.

Ingredients

•	flour	600g	• granulated sugar	10g
•	pork	600g	• soy sauce	10g
	(70% lean and 30% fat)		• sesame oil	4g
•	Chinese mushrooms	60g	• peanut oil	100g
•	salt	8g	• water	300g
•	MSG	5g		

Preparation

1. Pour just-boiled water into the flour and let it cool a little before kneading into a smooth dough. Cover with cloth and leave for 30 minutes. Dice the pork finely. Mix in salt, cooking wine and soy sauce. Add a little water and stir till springy. Add sugar, MSG and 10g peanut oil. Keep stirring in a single direction till springy. Finally, add diced mushrooms and sesame oil. 2. Shape the dough into long sticks. Cut into 12 portions of equal length. Shape into a ball and roll into flat circular skins. Wrap the filling in and close the opening in the middle. Flatten lightly and you have the raw pies. 3. Heat and brush a layer of oil in a saucepan, and place the pies in. Grill on low heat till the base is golden-brown. Brush the top with a layer of oil, flip, and grill till both sides are golden-brown. Serve.

Variations

LEEK PORK PIES – Simply substitute mushrooms with leek.

CHIVE PIES – Wash and cut chives into sections, and mix salt and vegetable oil for the filling.

BEEF PIES – Mix finely diced beef, spring onion, salt, oil and pepper for the filling.

GREEN PORK PIES – Prepare as above, adding some chive juice when kneading the dough.

PRAWN PEEL AND CABBAGE PIES – Dice cabbage finely and marinate with salt for 10 minutes. Squeeze out the excess moisture. Mix the cabbage with prawn peel, Sichuan peppercorns, salt, MSG, diced spring onion and diced ginger for the filling.

東北酸菜鍋餅 (dong1 bei3 suan1 cai4 guo1 bing3)
NORTHEASTERN SAUERKRAUT PIES

These pies are usually prepared in a single pot. They represent the taste of Northeastern China, with a crispy and golden-brown crust and a fragrant filling so abundant that it almost spills out.

Ingredients

• flour	500g	• salt	8g
• egg	5	• MSG	3g
• pork	300g	• soy sauce	10g
• sauerkraut (sour Chinese cabbage)	300g	• peanut oil	120g
• carrot	50g	• cold water	400g
• leek	50g	• starch	5g
• ginger	10g	• spring onion	20g

Preparation

1. Dice the pork finely. Squeeze the cabbage lightly to remove moisture. Wash and grate the carrot into strips. Dice spring onion and ginger. Mix all the above with salt, MSG, soy sauce and starch to get the filling. 2. Pour the flour and eggs into a large bowl. Add 300g water and stir with force. Add 100g water to get a paste. Heat a saucepan and wipe with a cloth dipped in oil. When the oil is 60% to boiling, scoop the paste in. Shake the saucepan lightly so that the paste covers the whole base so as to get an even skin. 3. Spread filling on the skin and wrap into a rectangle about 25cm long and 10cm wide. Scrape up the remaining skin to close the opening. Pour some peanut oil into the pan and grill till the pie base is golden-brown. Brush the top with a layer of oil, flip, and grill till both sides are golden-brown. Cut into small rectangles and serve.

Variations

BEAN PASTE PIES – Use red bean paste for the filling.

DATE PASTE PIES – Use red date paste for the filling.

PORK STRIP PIES – Cut pork into strips. Dip in a batter of starch and salt and stir-fry. Thicken the gravy with starch, remove and let dry. Mix with diced chives for the filling.

鹹酥餅 (xian2 su1 bing3)

SAVOURY PUFFS

Savoury Puffs originated from Beijing. They have many layers of flavour and have a light and puffy texture. The spring onion fragrance wafting from the puffs whets one's appetite.

Ingredients

•	flour	500g	• ginger	5g
•	vegetable oil	120g	• cumin	5g
•	leek	25g	• salt	5g
•	salt	10g	• pepper	5g
•	sichuan peppercorn	5g	• water	250g
•	spring onion	5g		

Preparation

1. Dice the spring onion and slice the ginger. Add 100g oil into a wok. Heat and add peppercorn, cumin, spring onion and ginger. Deep-fry till the spring onion changes colour, and scoop the ginger, cumin and peppercorns out. Let the oil cool, then add 80g flour, pepper and salt and mix to become the flaky skin. 2. Add salt to 25g cool water. Let it dissolve and pour the water into the remaining flour. Mix and knead into the skin dough. 3. Rub the dough into a stick about 3.5cm long and divide into 5 sections. Roll each section into a ball, then a large rectangular skin. Spread on a layer of the flaky skin mix, fold 3 times lengthwise then 3 times breadth wise. Roll out the folds to their original size, spread on another layer of flaky skin mix. Roll up from one side, and connect two ends of the long roll so you get a doughnut shape. Leave for 15 minutes. Roll and flatten into a round disc and sprinkle with sesame. 4. Heat a saucepan, and brush both sides of the dough with oil. Grill till the base is golden-brown. Flip and grill till both sides are golden-brown.

Variations

SAVOURY PUFFS WITH PORK FLOSS

– Prepare as above. After leaving the dough for 15 minutes, roll out the dough and wrap in pork floss. Rub into a ball and flatten. Grill and serve.

酒釀軟餅 (jiu3 niang4 ruan3 bing3)
SOFT PASTRIES WITH WINE LEES

These pastries are a specialty of Jiangnan (south of the river Yangtze), and consumed to celebrate the coming of spring. They are soft, chewy and sweet with a faint hint of wine.

Ingredients

- flour   500g
- wine lees   60g
- sugar   200g
- fresh yeast   40g
- sesame oil   50g

Preparation

1. Add yeast to warm water and stir. Pour in flour and add sugar and wine lees. Knead into dough. Cover with a wet cloth and leave for 2 hours. Rub the dough into sticks and break off small portions weighing about 100g each. Rub into balls and flatten. 2. Heat a saucepan and brush one side of the pastry with oil. Grill till the base is cooked. Flip and grill till both sides are burnt-red and bouncy.

Variations

PASTRIES WITH WINE LEES AND BEAN PASTE – Prepare as above, and wrap red bean paste into the dough.
PASTRIES WITH WINE LEES AND SUGAR FILLING – Stir-fry a little flour and mix with sugar for the filling.
PASTRIES WITH WINE LEES AND ROSE – Use rose jam as the filling.

黑芝麻油酥餅 (hei1 zhi1 ma2 you2 su1 bing3)
BLACK SESAME PUFFS

Black Sesame Puffs are light, puffy and full of sesame fragrance, making a very popular breakfast in Northern China.

Ingredients

• flour	500g
• vegetable oil	150g
• black sesame	50g
• salt	5g
• chicken essence	5g
• pepper	3g
• water	100g

Preparation

1. Grind 20g sesame into powder. Heat 80g oil in a wok and mix in the sesame powder. Add pepper, salt and chicken essence. Pour in 200g flour in 3 portions. Knead the mixture thoroughly into dough for the second skin. Knead the remaining 300g flour with 100g water and 70g oil into dough for the skin. Divide both skins into 5 portions each. 2. Roll out a portion of skin. Wrap in a portion of second skin and roll into a big rectangle. Fold 3 times lengthwise then 3 times breadth wise. Repeat the rolling and folding 2 times. Roll out and roll up from one side, connecting two ends of the long roll so you get a doughnut shape. Roll the dough out and flatten with your hands. Sprinkle on sesame. Repeat for the other puffs. 3. Heat a saucepan, brush with oil, and grill till both sides are golden-brown.

Variations

SWEET PUFFS – Prepare as above. Knead the skin using flour, sugar and vegetable oil. Sprinkle with white sesame instead.

五仁烙餅 (wu3 ren2 lao4 bing3)
ASSORTED NUT PIES

These pies are crispy and full of flavour, with a strong fragrance of sesame on the outside while the filling is smooth and substantial. The 5 types of nuts used in these pies represent the 5 principal virtues of traditional Chinese culture, namely benevolence, loyalty, manners, wisdom and honesty.

Ingredients

•	peanut	30g
•	pine nut	30g
•	walnut	30g
•	almond	30g
•	melon seed	30g
(above is namely, the 5 types of nuts)		
•	sesame oil	50g
•	yeast powder	50g
•	cooked lard	120g
•	sugar	120g
•	flour	550g
•	sesame	30g
•	water	250g

Preparation

1. Stir-fry the nuts till done, shell and dice. Add sugar, lard and 50g for the filling. 2. Mix water, 500g flour and rising powder. Knead into dough and leave for 10 minutes. Roll into long sticks and break off 20 portions. Flatten each portion and wrap the filling in, then flatten with your hand and sprinkle on sesame. 3. Heat a saucepan, brush with oil, and grill till both sides are golden-brown.

Variations

BEAN PASTE PIES – Substitute the five nuts with red bean paste for the filling.
YAM PASTE PIES – Wash, steam, skin and mash yams to make the filling.

葱油酥餅 (cong1 you2 su1 bing3)
SPRING ONION PUFFS

Spring Onion Puffs are one of the most famous Shanghai breakfast snacks that emits a strong spring onion fragrance. Crispy on the outside and light on the inside, the pastry layers of the puffs are as thin as cicada wings and they practically melt in the mouth.

Ingredients

- flour   240g
- cooked lard   100g
- vegetable oil   20g
- spring onions   30g
- salt   10g

Preparation

1. Dice spring onions. Mix 160g flour, 50g lard, salt, spring onion and warm water thoroughly and knead into a dough for the second skin. Knead 80g flour and 50g lard into dough for the skin. Divide both skins into 5 portions each. 2. Roll out a portion of skin, wrap in a portion of second skin, flatten and roll into a big rectangle. Cut off the parts with only 1 layer. Press the cut-off parts onto the rectangle. Roll up from one end and rub into a ball. Roll into a puff about 3cm wide and 10cm long. Repeat for the other portions. 3. Heat a saucepan, brush with oil, and grill till both sides are dark-yellow.

煎餅 (jian1 bing3)
CREPES

Crepes from Shandong are delicious and easy to make and they have won the hearts of many. These crepes are made with mixed grains, making them soft yet chewy. With the sweet bean sauce, chilli sauce, coriander and diced spring onions, its varied flavours can brighten up your day.

Ingredients

- green bean flour   300g
- millet flour   300g
- five-spice powder   50g
  (chilli, cumin, fennel seed,
  cassia and star anise)
- eggs   5
- sweet bean sauce   75g
- coriander   10g
- vegetable oil   30g

Preparation

1. Mix the 2 flours and add some water. Mix to get a thin paste. Stir in the five-spice powder. Dice coriander. 2. Heat a saucepan, brush on oil, and pour in a tablespoonful of the paste. Use a wooden spreader or metal spatula to spread the paste out into a circle. Beat in an egg and spread evenly. Spread 15g sweet bean sauce and 2g coriander. Fold into a rectangle, cut in the middle with the spatula and remove. Spread on chilli to taste.

Variations

CRISPY CREPES – Wrap a dough fritter or cracker into the crepe after it is done.

椒鹽烙餅 (jiao1 yan2 lao4 bing3)

PEPPERCORN SALT PANCAKES

These pancakes are soft and appetising with the unique blend of peppercorns and salt. They can be eaten alone or dipped in gravy.

Ingredients
- wheat flour   300g
- salt   10g
- spicy salt   20g
  (Sichuan peppercorns and salt)
- peanut oil   30g

Preparation

1. Mix the flour, salt, spicy salt and some water. Knead thoroughly into dough and rub into a long stick. Divide into 6 portions and flatten them. 2. Heat a saucepan, brush it with oil, and grill till the base is yellow. Flip, brush the other side with oil, and grill till both sides are yellow.

Variations

MILLET PANCAKES – Prepare as above, adding 500g of cooked millet to the dough.
ZUCCHINI PANCAKES – Remove the skin, pulp and seeds of the zucchini. Grate into thin strips. Mix with flour, eggs, chicken essence, salt and a little sesame oil, and grill as above.

肉夹馍 (rou4 jia1 mo2)
PORK IN POCKET BREAD

This Xi'an snack has won the hearts of many Chinese people. In many parts of Xi'an, you can see ancient black grills churning out snowy white and piping hot pockets of bread. Simply cut open the bread and put in some mouthwatering pork, and you have yourself a snack to savour.

Ingredients

• flour	300g
• yeast powder	20g
• lean pork	500g
• cassia bark	1g
• cumin	2g
• light soy sauce	100g
• sugar	10g
• salt	5g

Preparation

1. Dissolve the yeast in warm water. Pour into the flour and knead into dough. Cover with cloth and leave for an hour. Divide into 6 portions, shape into balls then flatten into breads about 1.5cm thick. Using a toothpick, poke small holes all over the dough. Heat a saucepan without oil and grill till the bread puffs up and both sides are light-yellow. Remember to keep flipping to prevent burning. 2. Slice the pork thinly and put in a pressure cooker. Add cassia bark, cumin powder, light soy sauce, sugar, salt and enough water to cover the meat. Stew on low heat for 25 minutes. If you open the cooker and find too much gravy, turn on high heat and cook till it thickens. Remove. 3. Cut open the bread from the middle without breaking it, and put the pork in.

Variations
DICED PORK IN POCKET BREAD – Take fatty pork, cook till soft and dice quickly. Put in the bread with a little gravy and diced coriander

春餅 (chun1 bing3)
SPRING WRAPS

In China, people traditionally eat these wraps at the start of spring. Chewy and filled with crunchy vegetables, these wraps symbolise hard work, vibrancy and staying power. They also bring the freshness of spring to your tastebuds.

Ingredients
- flour   100g
- water   30g
- cucumber   50g
- carrot   50g
- bean sprouts   50g
- salt   5g
- MSG   5g
- sesame oil   10g
- vegetable oil   30g

Preparation
1. Wash and grate the carrot and cucumber. Blanch the carrot strips and dry. Mix the carrot strips with the cucumber, salt, MSG and sesame oil. 2. Put the flour into a large bowl. Add hot water slowly and stir with chopsticks to get wisps of flour. When it has cooled slightly, hand-knead into dough. Cover with cloth and leave for 30 minutes. Rub into long sticks and divide into 4 equally-sized portions. Shape each portion into balls and flatten into circles. Brush one portion with a thin layer of oil and press another portion together to make the wrap. Heat a saucepan and place the wrap in. Grill on low heat till both sides are done. Separate the 2 halves and place the vegetables in before serving.

Variations
SPRING WRAPS WITH EGG – Simply add egg to the dough.
SPRING WRAPS WITH HAM – Slice, blanch and dry cabbage and onions. Mix cabbage and onions with sliced ham, sliced shepherd's purse, vinegar and salt. Wrap as above.

韭菜盒子 (jiu3 cai4 he2 zi)

CHIVE PIES

Despite its simple preparation, Chive Pies are fresh and succulent. The contrasting flavours are bound to leave a lasting impression on your tastebuds.

Ingredients

• chives	250g
• egg	3
• prawn shells	25g
• flour	500g
• hot water	300g
• salt	5g
• pepper	3g
• sesame oil	10g
• vegetable oil	30g

Preparation

1. Wash the chives and cut into 1.5cm-long sections. Stir-fry the eggs with oil in a wok, and cut into strips with the spatula. Mix the chives, egg, prawn shells, salt, pepper and sesame oil for the filling. 2. Pour hot water into the flour. Let it cool slightly and knead into dough. Break off small bits and roll into circular skins. Wrap the filling in and fold diagonally. Press into hemispherical pies. 3. Heat and brush a saucepan with oil and put the pies in. When one side turns light-yellow, flip and grill the other side till you get the same colour. Pour a little water into the pan, cover and remove after 2 minutes.

Variations

CELERY PIES – Substitute chives with celery.
MEAT PIES – Use pork and shelled prawns for the filling.

玉米餅 (yu4 mi3 bing3)

CORN PASTRIES

These healthy pastries are full of fibres and vitamins. The sweetness of corn is combined with the creamy fragrance of milk, and the texture is slightly rough and extremely chewy.

Ingredients
- corn grist   100g
- milk   50g
- egg   2
- baking soda   1g
- vegetable oil   30g

Preparation
Pour a little water into the grist. Mix and add egg yolks, milk and baking soda. Continue to stir. Pour into a mould, and grill in a saucepan brushed with oil till both sides turn dark-yellow.

九两餠 (jiu3 liang3 bing3)
'NINE" LIANG PASTRIES

Nine "liang" is a traditional Chinese measurement for 450 grams, with one "liang" being 50 grams. This snack was invented by the Chinese-muslim community, with a thin and crispy skin on the outside and a fragrant and light filling inside.

Ingredients

• flour	300g
• dry yeast powder	7g
• salt	8g
• milk	400g
• vegetable oil	25g

Preparation

1. Mix the yeast powder, salt and milk. Add 60g flour and mix well. Cover with a wet cloth and leave in a warm place for 25 minutes. Add 5g vegetable oil, salt and 120g flour. Knead thoroughly. Add in the remaining flour in 3 portions. Keep kneading throughout, till the surface is smooth and free of excess flour. Cover with a wet cloth and leave in a warm place for an hour till it doubles in size. 2. Flatten the dough lightly into a 5cm-thick lump. Using a chopstick, poke a few small holes on both sides. Put 10g oil in a saucepan, and grill the dough on low heat. Flip after 5 minutes. Brush on the remaining oil, pour 40g water in the pan, and cover. Grill on medium heat for 3 to 4 minutes till the water dries up and both sides are golden-brown. Remove, slice and serve.

叉燒时蔬卷 (cha1 shao1 shi2 shu1 juan3)
CHAR SIEW AND VEGETABLE WRAPS

Char Siew and Vegetable Wraps sport bright, attractive colours and are easy to make.

Ingredients

- flour   100g
- water   30g
- cucumber   40g
- carrot   40g
- char siew (barbecued pork)   20g
- vegetable oil   30g

Preparation

1. Wash and grate the carrot and cucumber. Blanch the carrot strips and dry. Cut the char siew into strips. 2. Add water to the flour to make a paste. Heat and brush a saucepan with oil and pour in the paste. Spread the paste evenly. When the paste hardens into a thin wrap, place some carrot, cucumber, char siew and wrap. Serve.

烤点

BAKED
DIM SUM

叉燒酥 (cha1 shao1 su1)
CHAR SIEW PUFFS

Char Siew Puffs are a popular Cantonese snack with crispy skins and tasty fillings.

Ingredients

For the skin:

•	all-purpose flour	150g
•	egg	1

For the second skin:

•	low-gluten flour	150g
•	lard	60g
•	cream	240g

For the meat filling:

•	char siew roasted meat	240g
•	char siew sauce	240g

Preparation

1. Buy ready-made char siew meat, slice and mix with char siew sauce to make the filling. Mix the all-purpose flour, 1 egg and water, and knead till it becomes springy. Set the skin aside for later use. 2. Hand mix the low-gluten flour, lard and cream. 3. Prepare a tray and spread on absorbent baking paper. Press the second skin into a rectangle measuring about 20cm by 30cm. Put into the freezer for 10 minutes. Remove and spread the skin on a layer of similar size, then freeze for another 10 minutes. Remove the tray and turn it upside down on the counter top, leaving the ingredients behind. Fold the 2 layers towards the middle so they are folded over 3 times, then roll flat. Repeat the folding and rolling 3 times, making the dough 1cm thick the last time. Cut into squares measuring 6cm by 6cm and put aside. 4. Take 1 square, put some meat filling in the middle, and fold into a triangle. Press the bottom flat, place in a baking tray, brush on some liquid yolk. Repeat for the other puffs. Bake in a 250°C oven for about 15 minutes, and serve.

Variations

CHEESE PUFFS – Prepare as above, substituting char siew with cheese.

MATCHA CHAR SIEW PUFFS – Prepare as above, but add matcha (green tea) powder into the fat filling, and you'll get char siew puffs imbued with the refreshing fragrance of green tea.

叉燒塔 (cha1 shao1 ta3)

CHAR SIEW TARTS

Char Siew Tarts combine the crispy skin of egg tarts with the delicious filling of char siew puffs to make a snack that is both sweet and savoury.

Ingredients

For the skin:

- low-gluten flour   270g
- high-gluten flour   30g
- shortening   45g
- sliced margarine   250g

For the filling:

- char siew meat   240g
- char siew sauce   240g

Preparation

1. Buy ready-made char siew meat, slice and mix with char siew sauce to make the filling. 2. Mix the low-gluten flour, high-gluten flour and shortening, and knead into dough, adding water bit by bit till the dough is smooth and shiny. Wrap in cling wrap and leave for 20 minutes. Wrap the margarine tightly in plastic and beat with a rolling pin, till it becomes thinner and as soft as the dough. Remove the plastic and set aside. 3. Spread a thin layer of flour on the counter top, and roll the dough into a flat rectangle, as wide as the margarine and 3 times longer. Place the margarine in the middle of the dough, and fold the 2 sides to wrap it up. Pinch one end shut, and starting from that end, press the dough with your palms. When you reach the other end, squeeze that shut too. Roll the dough out lengthwise, fold it like a blanket till it becomes 4 times as thick, and beat lightly with a rolling pin. Roll lengthwise and lightly beat once again. Roll into a rectangle, and fold four-fold again. Wrap in cling wrap and leave for 20 minutes. 4. Roll the dough out again into a piece 0.6cm thick, 20cm wide and 35-40cm long. Trim off the excess at the sides with a penknife. Roll up the dough, starting from the longer side. Wrap in cling wrap and freeze for 30 minutes. Cut the dough into pieces about 1cm thick each. Dip one side in flour, then place it in an un-oiled tart mould with floury side facing up. Use your thumbs to get the desired tart shape. 5. Put in the char siew filling and bake for 15 minutes at 220°C.

Variations

PORK AND ONION TARTS – see pg164
EGG TARTS – see pg164

蛋黄酥 (dan4 huang2 su1)
EGG YOLK PUFFS

Egg Yolk Puffs is a traditional snack which brings back memories of childhood. The puffs are not prepared with a lot of oil, and are thus healthier than Western-style puffs.

Ingredients

For the yolk filling:
- salted egg yolks   20g
- red bean paste   400g

For the skin:
- high-gluten flour   80g
- low-gluten flour   80g
- icing sugar   30g
- oil   55g

For the second skin:
- low-gluten flour   220g
- oil   90g

Others:
- egg york liquid   30g
- black sesame   a little
- some white wine

Preparation

1. Sprinkle some white wine on the salted egg yolks, and bake in a 180°C oven for 7 to 8 minutes till half done. Let it cool and set aside. Separate the red bean paste in 20 portions and set aside. 2. Mix all the ingredients for the second skin, knead into dough and separate into 20 portions. 3. Mix all the ingredients for the skin, knead into a smooth dough that doesn't stick to your hands, cover with cling wrap and leave for 20 minutes. Then separate into 20 portions, press flat, wrap the second skin portions in, and press the skin shut. Roll the skins lengthwise, then roll them up. Repeat the lengthening and rolling. Repeat for the other 19 portions. Cover the skins with cling wrap and leave for 20 minutes. 4. Flatten the 20 portions into flat circles. Place a little red bean paste in the middle, add a salted yolk, then put more bean paste, just enough to cover the yolk. Wrap it up like a bun, and press the opening shut. Adjust the shape, then place the puffs into a baking tray with openings facing down. Brush on egg yolk liquid and sprinkle on black sesame. Pre-heat an oven to 220°C and bake for 20 minutes till the puffs turn yellowish-brown.

Variations
PEA PASTE PUFFS – see pg165

豆沙卷 (dou4 sha1 juan3)

BEAN PASTE ROLLS

Popular with the young and old, Bean Paste Rolls look appealing with their soft textures and crispy skins.

Ingredients

For the fillings:
- red bean paste   400g

For the skin:
- high-gluten flour   80g
- low-gluten flour   80g
- icing sugar   30g
- oil   55g

For the second skin:
- low-gluten flour   220g
- oil   90g

Others
- egg york liquid   30g

Preparation

1. Mix all the ingredients for the skin, knead into a smooth dough that doesn't stick to your hands, cover with cling wrap and leave for 20 minutes. 2. Mix all the ingredients for the second skin, knead into dough and separate into 20 portions. 3. Roll the skins lengthwise, then roll them up. Repeat the lengthening and rolling. Repeat for the other 19 portions. Cover the skins with cling wrap and leave for 20 minutes. 4. Roll the skins into long pieces, put in the bean paste, wrap up and knead evenly. Cut the rolls into pieces about 6cm long each, and cut 2 holes in each for the bean paste to peek through. Place into a baking tray and brush on egg yolk liquid. Pre-heat an oven to 220°C and bake for 20 minutes till the puffs turn golden-brown.

Variations

RED DATE ROLLS – Wash, cook, skin and seed some red dates. Wrap into the puff skins and bake.

SESAME ROLLS – Prepare as above, but use a mixture of lard and black sesame for the filling.

瓜仁脆餅 (gua1 ren2 cui4 bing3)
SUNFLOWER SEED CRACKERS

Among the common baked pastries, Sunflower Seed Crackers are the easiest to prepare and with some creativity, you can make even more appealing crackers.

Ingredients

- egg   2
- icing sugar   100g
- low-gluten flour   18g
- corn starch   12g
- salad oil   25g
- sunflower seeds   80g
- vanilla powder   1g

Preparation

1. Add icing sugar to the eggs and beat till the sugar dissolves, then mix in the salad oil. Run the flour, starch and vanilla powder through a sieve and mix in, and finally add in the sunflower seeds. Spread a layer of baking powder on the baking tray, and scoop the mixture on. Do not let the circles of mixture touch each other. 2. Pre-heat the oven for 10 minutes to 170°C. Place the tray into the upper part of the oven and turn the oven on to full heat. After 8 to 10 minutes, the crackers are ready to serve.

Variations
MELON SEED CRACKERS – see pg165

PORK AND ONION TARTS
(Yang2 Cong1 Yan1 Rou4 Ta3)

Preparation
Dice some onions and cured pork, and stir-fry
on low heat till done. Substitute for the char
siew and prepare as pg157.

EGG TARTS
(Dan4 Ta3)

Preparation
Prepare 100g cream, 200g milk, 60g sugar, 4
egg yolks and 25ml condensed milk. Boil the
cream, milk, condensed milk and sugar in a
small pot, let it cool and add in the beaten egg
yolks. Pour into the tart skin and bake as pg157.

PEA PASTE PUFFS
(Dou4 Ni2 Su1)

Preparation
Wash and skin 250g of peas, and mash into a paste. Heat a wok, pour in cooked lard, then stir-fry the paste till it becomes dry and doesn't stick to the wok. Add in sugar and salt, and fry till all the sugar has melted. Wrap into the puff skins as above, and bake till the puffs turn yellowish-brown. See pg158.

MELON SEED CRACKERS
(Gua1 Ren2 Su1 Pian4)

Preparation
Mix low-gluten flour with butter and icing sugar, wrap in cling wrap and freeze. Remove, roll it to 3mm thickness and cut into rectangles. Sprinkle on shelled melon seeds and brush on a layer of butter, then bake. See pg162.

海棠糕 (hai3 tang2 gao1)

CRABAPPLE CAKES

Crabapple Cakes are a traditional Shanghai snack that have endured the test of time. Shaped like crabapple blossoms, donned with a scarlet purple colour, these cakes are equally outstanding in fragrance and taste.

Ingredients

- flour   2000g
- red bean paste   500g
- yeast   150g
- baking soda   50g
- lard   100g
- sugar   100g
- peanut oil   75g

Preparation

1. Dissolve the baking soda in 50g of water. Similarly, mix water to the peanut oil. Dice the lard into 80 pieces, add 100g of sugar and mix. 2. Pour the flour into a basin, make into a paste with cold water, and add the yeast. Add some baking soda solution till the paste is not acidic and yellow. Heat the cake moulds, brush on a little watered-down oil, and half-fill it with flour paste. Add 20g of red bean paste into every mould, and pour in some more paste till the bean paste is covered. Place in one piece of sugared lard, and bake for about 5 minutes. 3. Sprinkle some sugar into some metal plates. Remove the cakes from the moulds, and place them upside down on the plates. Heat the plates over fire till the sugar melts. Flip the cakes over and serve.

黑芝麻三角酥 (hei1 zhi1 ma2 san1 jiao3 su1)
SESAME TRIANGULAR PUFFS

Since black sesame is a healthy and nutritious food, a black pastry dish is, naturally, a guilt-free indulgence.

Ingredients

For the fillings:
- black sesame   500g
- sugar   200g
- cooked lard   20g

For the skin:
- high-gluten flour   80g
- low-gluten flour   80g
- icing sugar   30g
- oil   55g

For the second skin:
- low-gluten flour   220g
- oil   90g

Others:
- egg yolk liquid   30g

Preparation

1. Stir-fry the sesame on low heat till done. Put 50g aside and mash the rest into powder. Mix with sugar and lard to make the sesame paste filling. 2. Mix all the ingredients for the second skin, knead into dough and separate into 20 portions. 3. Mix all the ingredients for the skin, knead into a smooth dough that doesn't stick to your hands, cover with cling wrap and leave for 20 minutes. Separate into 20 portions and wrap the second skin in. 4. Roll the skins lengthwise, then roll them up. Repeat the lengthening and rolling. Repeat for the other 19 portions. Cover the skins with cling wrap and leave for 20 minutes. 5. Roll the skins into squares and using a mould or knife, remove the excess skin. Place the filling in, fold diagonally corner-to-corner and place in a baking tray. Repeat for the other puffs. Brush on liquid yolk, sprinkle on black sesame. Pre-heat an oven to 200°C and bake for 20 minutes till the puffs turn golden-brown.

Variations

SPICY SALT TRIANGULAR PUFFS – Prepare as above, substituting the filling for a thin layer of spicy salt (powdered Sichuan peppercorns with salt) on the insides of the skins.

CURRY PUFFS – Dice chicken, stir-fry on high heat, add in curry sauce and salt. Use this as the filling.

烘番薯片 (hong1 fan1 shu3 pian4)
BAKED TAPIOCA CHIPS

Potato chips are a popular snack amongst many but some do not know that chips can be easily made at the convenience of your home simply from potato or tapioca.

Ingredients
For the skin:

• tapioca	500g
• juice of lemon	1
• olive oil	20g
• salt	5g

Preparation
Wash, skin and thinly slice the tapioca. Place the slices in a flat receptacle, and marinate in lemon juice, olive oil and salt for 1 to 2 hours. Drain the slices and bake at 40°C for 6 to 8 hours.

老北京喜字餅 (lao3 bei3 jing1 xi3 zi4 bing3)
BEIJING WEDDING CAKES

These cakes are one of the traditional snacks of old Beijing and is a popular feature at weddings for commoners and officials alike. Their exquisite look and taste is quite unlike other snacks.

Ingredients
- flour   500g
- sugar   50g
- cooked lard   20g
- egg   2
- red dates   500g
- brown sugar   50g
- cooked peabut oil   20g
- liquid yolk   20g

Preparation

1. Mix the sugar and lard, then stir in the egg. Add flour and water after. Stir and knead into dough. 2. Wash and boil the red dates till they soften, let them cool, skin and seed. Continue cooking the red date flesh till they absorb all the water, and then dissolve the brown sugar in the pot. Add peanut oil in several portions, and mix thoroughly till the red dates become a paste. Divide the dough into 10 portions, flatten and wrap in the filling. Put into a mould with the character '喜' (happiness) carved in it. Remove and place on a baking tray, then brush with liquid yolk. Pre-heat the oven to 200°C and bake for 15 minutes. Serve.

老婆餅 (lao3 po2 bing3)
"WIFE PASTRIES"

"Wife Pastries" are a traditional Cantonese snack. They are basically round cookies in flaky skins. The coconut-flavoured filling is sweet without being saccharine, and is best when savoured freshly out of the oven.

Ingredients

For the skin:

- low-gluten flour   200g
- high-gluten flour   50g
- sugar   10g
- lard   30g

For the second skin:

- low-gluten flour   220g
- butter   110g

For the fillings:

- glutinous rice flour   225g
- desiccated coconut   50g
- butter   40g
- lard   20g
- sugar   70g

Others

- liquid york   20g
- white sesame   15g

Preparation

1. Pre-heat an oven to 150°C, and bake the glutinous rice flour in a tray for 10 minutes. Blend with the other filling ingredients, cover with cling wrap and set aside. 2. Mix 200g low-gluten flour and 50g high-gluten flour, then add in 10g sugar and 30g lard, knead into dough, cover with cling wrap and set aside. 3. Mix the 220g low-gluten flour and 110g butter, and slowly pinch and squeeze with your hands till they are blended into dough. 4. Separate the skin dough, second skin dough and filling into the same number of portions. Each skin portion should weigh 28g, each second skin portion 20g and each filling portions 25g. 5. For each pastry, wrap a second skin portion into a skin portion. Roll the skins lengthwise, then roll them up. Repeat the lengthening and rolling. Repeat for the other 19 portions. Cover the skins with cling wrap and leave for 20 minutes. 6. Lightly flatten a lump of blended dough with your palm, then roll into a flat circle. Wrap the filling in, place it with opening facing down and flatten a little with your palm. Roll into a cookie about 0.8 to 1cm thick. Brush on liquid yolk, sprinkle on white sesame and bake. Pre-heat an oven to 190°C and bake for 20 minutes. Serve.

蓮蓉月餅 (lian1 rong2 yue4 bing3)
LOTUS PASTE MOONCAKES

The Mid-Autumn Festival is a festival celebrated amongst Chinese around the world, and so is the tradition of eating mooncakes during the festival. Mooncakes are not only delicious but they also symbolise the wish for a reunited family.

Ingredients

•	peanut oil	300g	• lotus seeds	500g
•	low-gluten flour	600g	• sugar	200g
•	syrup	350g	• lemon juice	10g
•	baking soda solution	300g		

Preparation

1. Wash and soak the lotus seeds, remove the core and boil till it turns mushy. Blend into a paste using a blender. Stir-fry the lotus seeds with sugar and when it has dried out, add in a little peanut oil. Keep stir-frying till the paste doesn't stick to your ladle. Mix in lemon juice, cool and set aside. 2. Pour the oil slowly, over 4 to 6 pourings, into a syrup-filled container. Keep stirring so the colour is even and the syrup doesn't bubble. Pour in some baking soda solution to improve the texture and colour. Then stir in some flour, stirring for about 10 minutes till you can't see any raw flour and the colour is even. Remove the dough from container, cover with cling wrap and leave for 15 to 20 minutes. Sprinkle some flour on a chopping board, and cut the dough into small portions. Shape into flat circles, slightly thicker in the middle. 3. Put a ball of filling into the dough, wrap evenly from top to bottom and close the opening. Put into a mooncake mould and flatten lightly and evenly with your hand. Hit the moulds in order for the mooncakes to attain a standard shape. 4. Place the mooncakes in an oven, and set the heat to 50 to 100°C for the bottom and 200°C for the top. After 5 minutes, remove the mooncakes, brush on liquid yolk, flip the baking tray lengthwise and return to oven. Raise the temperature to 220°C and bake for another 20 to 30 minutes, till the mooncakes turn golden-brown. Remove and serve.

Variations

MIXED-FRUIT MOONCAKES – Mix flour (stir-fried till done), sugar, vegetable oil, 1 tablespoon of honey, sugared kumquats (diced to the size of soy beans), shelled walnuts (diced to the size of green beans), pine nuts, sesame and shelled melon seeds for the filling. Otherwise, prepare as above.

COCONUT MOONCAKES – Prepare as above, but use coconut paste for the filling.
ROSE AND RED BEAN MOONCAKES – Prepare as above, but use red bean paste with rose essence for the filling.

玫瑰花生酥 (mei2 gui4 hua1 sheng1 su1)
ROSY PEANUT PUFFS

Rosy Peanut Puffs are a snack that taste slightly powdery on the inside. The rose petal jam in the filling makes the puffs fragrant with a silky smooth texture.

Ingredients

- rose petal jam   100g
- red bean paste   200g
- shelled peanuts   600g
- sugar   200g

Preparation

1. Mix the rose petal jam and red bean paste evenly. 2. Stir-fry the peanuts till they are yellowish and crispy, remove from fire and cool. Rub off the peanut skins. Mix the peanuts with sugar and crush into powder. Add the crushed peanuts till the mould is 1/3 full, then fill 1/3 with your blended paste, and the last 1/3 with the peanuts again. 3. Press tightly, shake a little, remove from moulds and serve.

Variations

DATE AND PEANUT PUFFS – Prepare as above, substituting red bean paste with red date paste.

COCONUT PEANUT PUFFS – Prepare as above, substituting red bean paste with coconut paste.

肉丁燒餅 (rou4 ding1 shao1 bing3)
PORK PIES

Pork Pies have been around for a very long time. Golden-brown and comfortingly fat, and they are best eaten hot.

Ingredients

For the filling:

• fresh pork	300g
• fresh ginger	5g
• salt	10g
• oil	20g

For the skin:

• all-purpose flour	500g
• yeast powder	10g

For the second skin:

• low-gluten flour	250g
• lard	30g

Others:

• sesame	30g

Preparation

1. Wash and dice the pork. Dice the ginger. Stir-fry them both in oil until 70% done, add some salt and put aside. 2. Take the ingredients for the skin and knead into dough. Let it ferment for an hour, then knead till smooth. Divide the dough into 20 portions. 3. Stir-fry the low-gluten flour with sugar till done, then mix it with lard to make a paste. Divide into 20 portions. 4. Wrap the second skin in the skin, then flatten and wrap in the filling. Flatten to make a pie, brush on water and sprinkle on sesame. Preheat the oven to 200°C, bake the pies for 20 minutes and serve.

Variations

SWEET PIES – Prepare as above, using sugar and osmanthus in place of the pork filling.
SPICY SALT PIES – Prepare as above, using spicy salt (powdered Sichuan peppercorns with salt) in place of the pork filling.

肉松卷 (rou4 song1 juan3)
PORK FLOSS ROLLS

These are prepared very much the same way as bean paste rolls but with a very different taste. The pork floss becomes even fluffier after baking and its fragrance soaks thoroughly into the skin, making the rolls even more appealing than the usual.

Ingredients
For the filling:
- pork floss   400g
- sugar   200g
- cooked lard   20g

For the skin:
- low-gluten flour   80g
- high-gluten flour   80g
- icing sugar   30g
- oil   55g

For the second skin:
- low-gluten flour   220g
- oil   90g

Others:
- sesame   30g
- liquid yolk   30g

Preparation
1. Mix all the ingredients for the skin, knead into a smooth dough that doesn't stick to your hands, cover with cling wrap and leave for 20 minutes. Separate into 20 portions and press flat. 2. Mix all the ingredients for the second skin, knead into dough and separate into 20 portions. 3. Wrap the second skins in the skins, closing the openings tightly. Roll the skins lengthwise, then roll them up. Repeat the lengthening and rolling. Repeat for the other 19 portions. Cover the skins with cling wrap and leave for 20 minutes. 4. Roll the skins into rectangles, cover with a layer of pork floss, and roll them up tightly. Cut them into pieces about 10cm long each, brush on liquid yolk and sprinkle on sesame. Bake in a pre-heated 200°C oven for 20 minutes till the rolls turn golden-brown, and serve.

蒜蓉焗馒头 (suan4 rong2 ju2 man2 tou2)

GARLIC BUNS

With a little effort, leftover mantou buns can be turned into a whole new delicious baked snack.

Ingredients

For the skin:

• small mantou buns	20g
• diced garlic	20g
• diced spring onions	30g
• cooking oil	20g

Preparation

Lightly stir-fry the garlic and spring onions till the garlic emits a strong fragrance. Remove and brush onto the buns. Bake the buns at 150°C for 10 minutes and serve.

螺絲轉 (luo2 si1 zhuan4)
BAKED SPIRALS

Baked Spirals are one of the most well-known snacks from Northern China, and are named after their spiral shape. They are not only distinctive in shape, but also in flavour.

Ingredients

- flour   500g
- sesame sauce   100g
- vegetable oil   50g
- fine salt   10g
- sichuan peppercorn   5g
- cumin   2g
- baking soda   10g
- fermented dough   150g
- liquid yolk   20g

Preparation

1. Mix the flour with water, and knead into dough. Cover with a wet cloth and leave for an hour. Add the baking soda and knead until the dough no longer tastes sour. Divide the dough into 20 portions, rub into long sticks, and roll into long rectangles. Rub on the sesame sauce, vegetable oil, fine salt, Sichuan peppercorn and cumin. Roll up, and press lightly. Cut the roll in half. With the cut surface facing down, press 2 rolled strips together. Taking an end in each hand, pull the dough into a long strip. Using one thumb as the "epicenter", twirl the strip around the center in one direction till it forms a spiral. 2. Brush the spirals with liquid yolk, place into the oven pre-heated to 230°C. bake for 15 to 20 minutes till they turn golden-brown.

Variations

PEANUT SPIRALS – Prepare as above, using peanut butter for the filling.
BEAN PASTE SPIRALS – Prepare as above, using red bean paste for the filling.
DATE PASTE SPIRALS – Prepare as above, using red date paste for the filling.

枣花酥 (zao3 hua1 su1)
RED DATE PUFFS

Red Date Puffs are another old Beijing snack. They look exquisite, and is a must-have on the menu for festivals and celebrations.

Ingredients

For the filling:
- red dates   500g
- brown sugar   50g
- cooked peanut oil   20g

For the skin:
- low-gluten flour   80g
- high-gluten flour   80g
- icing sugar   30g
- oil   55g

For the second skin:
- low-gluten flour   220g
- oil   90g

Others:
- amaranth juice   20g

Preparation

1. Wash the dates and boil on medium heat till mushy, let them cool and remove the seeds. Put the dates back into the pot till they absorb all the water, dissolve brown sugar in the paste and pour in the oil bit by bit. Mix the ingredients into a paste and set aside. 2. Mix all the ingredients for the skin, knead into a smooth dough that doesn't stick to your hands, cover with cling wrap and leave for 20 minutes. Separate into 20 portions and press flat. 3. Mix all the ingredients for the second skin, knead into dough and separate into 20 portions. 4. Wrap the second skins in the skins, closing the openings tightly. Roll the skins lengthwise, then roll them up. Repeat the lengthening and rolling. Repeat for the other 19 portions. Cover the skins with cling wrap and leave for 20 minutes. 5. Using moulds, cut the dough into the shape of a flower, put some red date paste in the middle, and dab on a little amaranth juice for decoration. Pre-heat the oven to 200°C, bake the pastries in a tray for 20 minutes and serve.

南瓜餅 (nan2 gua1 bing3)
PUMPKIN PASTRIES

Pumpkin Pastries are an extremely popular snack and can be prepared in many different ways. In this recipe, the pastry is baked to a soft flakiness, and is sweet yet refreshing to the taste.

Ingredients
For the filling:
- pumpkin   400g
- honey   30g

For the skin:
- low-gluten flour   80g
- high-gluten flour   80g
- icing sugar   30g
- oil   55g

For the second skin:
- low-gluten flour   220g
- oil   90g

Preparation
1. Wash, skin, seed and dice the pumpkin. Steam till done and mash, then simply stir in the honey and you have your filling. 2. Mix all the ingredients for the skin, knead into a smooth dough that doesn't stick to your hands, cover with cling wrap and leave for 20 minutes. Separate into 20 portions and press flat. 3. Mix all the ingredients for the second skin, knead into dough and separate into 20 portions. 4. Wrap the second skins in the skins, closing the openings tightly. Roll the skins lengthwise, then roll them up. Repeat the lengthening and rolling. Repeat for the other 19 portions. Cover the skins with cling wrap and leave for 20 minutes. 5. Shape the skins into flat circles, wrap some filling in. Shape them like buns and place on the baking tray, openings facing downwards. Bake in a pre-heated 200°C oven for 20 minutes till the pastries turn golden-brown, and serve.

煮点

BOILED
DIM SUM

裹蒸棕 (guo3 zheng1 zong4)

STEAMED RICE PYRAMIDS

Steamed Rice Pyramids are a specialty of Guangdong province, with the most famous ones originating from Zhaoqing province. Compared to regular rice pyramids, they contain much more varied fillings. and emit an enticing smell just out of the pot. They are moist but not too oily, chewy but not too sticky, and is a delicious blend of sweet and savoury.

Ingredients

•	glutinous rice	500g
•	green beans	250g
•	fatty pork	200g
•	dried lotus seeds	20g
•	chestnuts	20g
•	fresh shiitake mushrooms	20g
•	salted egg yolk	50g
•	barbecued char siew meat	50g
•	roasted duck	50g
•	ham	50g

•	water lilly leaves	5-7
•	wrapping leaves	20-30

(the origin of these leaves differs by region, you can also replaced with plantain leaves)

•	rice wine	20g
•	salt	3g
•	soy sauce	20g
•	cotton thread	

Preparation

1. Cook the water lily leaves in hot water for 5 minutes, wash and dry. Soak the wrapping leaves to soften, wash and dry. Soak the glutinous rice for an hour. Soak the green beans overnight, rub off the skin and dry. Soak the lotus seeds for an hour. Shell and wash the chestnuts, cook till they become mushy and set aside. Wash the pork, cut into small cubes. Remove the stems from the mushrooms, wash, dry and dice. Marinate the pork and mushrooms in salt, soy sauce and rice wine for half an hour. Cut the char siew meat, duck and ham into small cubes. Dice the salted egg yolk. 2. Take one water lily leaf, cover with 4 wrapping leaves, and cover with a layer of glutinous rice, then a layer of green beans. Place the pork, ham, char siew meat, duck, mushrooms, chestnuts, lotus seeds and salted egg yolk on. Cover with a layer of green beans, then a layer of glutinous rice. Wrap into a square-based pyramid, tie with cotton thread, and cook in boiling water for 3 hours. Remove and serve.

Variations

BEIJING RICE PYRAMIDS – Using glutinous rice or glutinous millet, wrap up cooked red dates and red bean paste, and wrap into a square or triangular-based pyramid and steam.

SICHUAN RICE PYRAMIDS – Soak red beans and glutinous rice for 5 hours, drain, and add in chilli powder, salt from Sichuan, MSG and a little cured meat. Wrap into rectangular-based dumplings and steam.

豬肉餃子 (zhu1 rou4 jiao3 zi)
PORK DUMPLINGS

Pork Dumplings are easy to prepare, and hence commonly made in Chinese homes. They have thin and smooth skins with tender and tasty fillings, and are usually served as a festive dish during Chinese New Year as it bodes a smooth and prosperous year ahead.

Ingredients
- wheat flour   400g
  (or ready-made dumpling skins)
- coriander   250g
- pork   150g
  (with both lean and fatty parts)
- light soy sauce   15g
- cooking wine   15g
- salt   3g
- MSG   1g
- sesame oil   2g

Preparation
1. Knead the flour with water, divide into portions of equal sizes, and roll into flat circles. Alternatively, you can use ready-made dumpling skins. 2. Wash the coriander, drain and dice, then mix in some sesame oil. Dice the pork into a paste, add light soy sauce, cooking wine, salt, MSG, sesame oil, and mix well. Then mix in the coriander to complcte making the filling. The pork should ideally have 30% fat and 70% lean meat. 3. Wrap the filling in the skins, and cook in boiling water.

Variations
MUTTON DUMPLINGS – Dice mutton into a paste, add diced ginger, diced spring onions, soy sauce, cooking wine, fine salt, pepper, peppercorn water (water in which peppercorns have been boiled and soaked) and liquid egg. Mix well, then add in sesame oil, peanut oil, and diced yellow chives or diced coriander to make the filling. Wrap the filling in the skins, and cook in boiling water.

FISH AND CHIVES DUMPLINGS – Prepare as above, but for the filling, substitute with 200g fish paste and 30g fatty pork. Mix with the seasonings as above together with diced chives.

蓮子八寶粥 (lian2 zi3 ba1 bao3 zhou1)
"EIGHT TREASURES" PORRIDGE WITH LOTUS SEEDS

Many Chinese families cook "eight treasures" porridge for the Winter Solstice to honour their ancestors and worship Buddha. Prepared with a large variety of ingredients, it is not only delicious, but also very nutritious and contains anti-aging properties.

Ingredients
- fragrant rice   100g
- glutinous rice   100g
- lotus seeds   20g
- green beans   20g
- red beans   20g
- cordyceps   20g
- peanuts   20g
- red dates   20g
- sugar   50g

Preparation
1. Soak the dates in cold water for 20 minutes. Wash, and steam for 30 minutes with the lotus seeds, green beans, red beans, cordyceps and peanuts. 2. Wash the rice and glutinous rice, and cook on low heat for 40 minutes. Add in the other ingredients and sugar, and cook till it becomes a mushy porridge.

Variations

"EIGHT TREASURES" PORRIDGE WITH CORN – Soak corn, peanuts, red beans and green beans. Add water and boil at high pressure. Add in pieces of pumpkin and red dates, then boil. Add in pieces of Jew's ear and shelled longan, and boil again. Serve.

BLACK RICE "EIGHT TREASURES" PORRIDGE – Soak cordyceps, oatmeal and lotus seeds in warm water, then add in black glutinous rice, white glutinous rice, red dates, shelled pine nuts, longans and rock sugar. Add water and cook on low heat for 90 minutes. Serve.

一口豆沙棕 (yi1 kou3 dou4 sha1 zong4)
MINI BEAN PASTE RICE PYRAMIDS

Mini Bean Paste Rice Pyramids are so tiny, you can finish them in a single bite. In that one bite, you can taste the combined leafy fragrance of glutinous rice together with the refreshing sweetness of bean paste.

Ingredients
- glutinous rice   250g
- wrapping leaves   10g
  (the origin of these leaves differ by region, you can use plantain leaves)
- bean paste   50g
- sugar   10g
- white lard   4g

Preparation
1. Wash the glutinous rice, soak for an hour, and mix in the sugar and lard. Cook the leaves in boiling water till they turn green. Drain, wash and soak for a while in cold water. 2. Take one leaf, shape into a pyramidal hollow. Put in the glutinous rice, followed by some bean paste, then cover with glutinous rice, and wrap into a square-based thin pyramid. Repeat for the other leaves. 3. Put the pyramids into a pot of boiling water, with the water about 1.5cm higher than the tips of the pyramids, and cook for 3 hours. Then raise them above the water, and stew them for 4 to 5 hours.

Variations
MINI SUGAR RICE PYRAMIDS – Prepare as above without the bean paste. When serving, dip in soft white sugar.
SAVOURY MINI RICE PYRAMIDS – Prepare as above, substituting diced ham for the bean paste, and 5g salt and 4g soy sauce for the sugar.

家鄉火鴨粥 (jia1 xiang1 huo3 ya1 zhou1)
HOMETOWN DUCK PORRIDGE

Cantonese people love porridge no matter the ingredients and preparation method. This style of duck porridge removes the oiliness of roast duck and is a healthy choice for modern city-dwellers. For some people, it can even bring back the warmth of home and memories from childhood.

Ingredients

• roast duck	1500g
• non-glutinous rice	150g
• spring onions	3g
• coriander	5g
• light soy sauce	2g
• lard	3g

Preparation

1. Cut the duck into pieces. Pour the rice into boiling water, boil on high heat, then stew on low heat. Wash and dice the spring onions and coriander. 2. When the rice grains have broken, add the duck and cook for 10 minutes, then mix in the spring onions, coriander, light soy sauce and lard. Stew for a while more and serve.

Variations

PORRIDGE SHEEP BONES – Mash the sheep bones, add in 5g mandarin orange peel, 5g tsaoko fruit and 50g fresh ginger. Cook these on low heat to a juice, sieve and cook with rice to get porridge. When serving, add salt to taste while the porridge is still hot.

BEEF PORRIDGE – Wash and slice beef, add in baking soda, cooking wine, fine salt, soy sauce, sugar, corn starch and some water, and mix well. Boil water, add non-glutinous rice, and cook into a porridge. Add the beef and boil on high heat. Add MSG, diced ginger and diced spring onions. Sprinkle on sesame oil and serve.

QUAIL PORRIDGE – Wash the quail and cut into pieces. Put the quail, rice and a little salt into boiling water, and cook on high heat.

港式鮮蝦雲吞 (gang4 shi4 xian1 xia1 yun2 tun1)
HONG KONG PRAWN WONTON

"Wonton" is the Cantonese term for dumplings. They are mostly random in shape, and the skins are simply gathered together to close any openings. These wontons stand out because they each include a whole prawn and are springy and incredibly succulent.

Ingredients

• wonton skin	240g	• egg	1
• peeled prawns	240g	• sesame oil	5g
• pork loin	320g	• pepper	2g
• corn starch	3g	• stock	500g
• salt	3g	(cooked with halibut, chicken and pig bones)	

Preparation

1. Mix the corn starch, salt, egg and pepper for the marinade. Wash and dry the prawns, then marinate for 10 minutes. Wash and dice the pork finely. Mix prawn and pork together for the filling.
2. Take one prawn and some pork, and wrap into a skin. Repeat for the other dumplings. Put them in boiling water and cook until they start to float. Pour in a bowl of cold water, and wait for the water to boil again. Remove the wontons. Serve with stock and sesame oil.

Variations

PORK WONTON – Dice pork with 30% fat and 70% lean meat into a paste and wrap into wonton skins. Cook the wontons till they float.

水蟹海鮮一品粥 (shui3 xie4 hai3 xian1 yi1 pin3 zhou1)
PREMIUM CRAB AND SEAFOOD PORRIDGE

Bright-orange crab shell bathed in white, smooth porridge – this dish is almost a work of art. The lip-smacking crab taste is imbued throughout the porridge, together with the abundant nutrition of the crab.

Ingredients

•	flower crab	1
•	rice	40g
•	ginger	5g
•	spring onion	5g
•	salt	2g
•	chicken essence	1g
•	sesame oil	5g

Preparation

1. Wash the crab and open up its shell. Cut the meat into pieces and smash the pincers with the back of a knife. Wash the rice. Cut the ginger into strips and dice the spring onion. 2. Using a clay pot, add in 2 parts rice and 8 parts water, boil on high heat, and then stew on low heat. Cook till the grains become mushy, add in ginger and crab, and cook to a porridge. Stir in chicken essence and salt, pour in sesame oil, sprinkle on diced spring onion and serve with the crabshell.

薺菜豬肉大餛飩 (qi2 cai4 zhu1 rou4 da4 hun2 tun)
PORK DUMPLINGS WITH SHEPHERD'S PURSE

Shepherd's purse has a unique and refreshing taste. Dumplings made from it are savoury, delicious and substantial, making it a very popular household food.

Ingredients

•	shepherd's purse	1500g
•	dumpling skin	1300g
•	pork	750g
	(with 30% fat and 70% lean meat)	
•	yellow wine	25g
•	salt	40g
•	granulated sugar	25g
•	sesame oil	50g
•	MSG	15g
•	lard	40g
•	coriander	2g

Preparation

1. Dice the pork finely. Dice the shepherd's purse. Mix with yellow wine, salt, granulated sugar, lard and MSG. Stir in the same direction till the mixture becomes resistant to stirring, and you have the filling. 2. Wrap the filling in the skins and cook till done in boiling water. Serve with the soup, some salt, sesame oil, and cut coriander.

Variations

PORK DUMPLINGS WITH CHIVES – Prepare as above, substituting shepherd's purse with green or yellow chives.

PORK DUMPLINGS – Prepare as above. Simply mix the pork with egg and seasonings for the filling.

CHICKEN DUMPLINGS – Prepare as above, substituting shepherd's purse with cooked strips of chicken.

"THREE TASTES" DUMPLINGS – Prepare as above. Simply mix pork, strips of scrambled egg, strips of dried tofu, black carp, peeled prawns and seasonings for the filling.

PORK DUMPLINGS WITH CABBAGE – Prepare as above, substituting shepherd's purse with cabbage. Dice the cabbage, wrap in gauze, and squeeze the extra moisture out.

鯪魚球粥 (ling2 yu2 qiu2 zhou1)
MUD CARP FISHBALL PORRIDGE

Mud carp fishballs are chewy and delicious, without any hint of unpleasant fishy smell. They can boost vitality levels and are good for the blood.

Ingredients

• rice	250g
• mud carp	500g
• pork	50g
• corn starch	50g
• salt	15g
• sesame oil	2g
• yellow wine	15g
• spring onion	2g
• ginger	2g

Preparation

1. Wash the rice, and mix with a little salt. Pour in boiling water and cook into a porridge. Wash the carp, and remove everything except the flesh. Pan-fry the fish parts till fragrant. Cook and pour the soup into the porridge. 2. Mix the fish flesh with corn starch, salt and yellow wine. Stir clockwise till the mixture becomes jelly-like. Beat the paste till it becomes springy, and shape into fishballs. Add into the porridge. 3. When the fishballs are cooked, sprinkle on diced spring onion and ginger strips and serve.

Variations
LUNG-NOURISHING FISH PORRIDGE

– Take the stock of crab, and boil. Add rice and boil again. Stew on low heat for 40 minutes. Add salt to taste. Take salmon and slice thinly, removing all the bones. Place in a bowl, and pour in the boiling hot porridge. Sprinkle on diced spring onion and pepper and serve.

潮式鲂鱼肉碎泡饭 (chao2 shi4 fang1 yu2 rou4 sui4 pao4 fan4)

TEOCHEW RICE IN FISH AND PORK SOUP

Add a variety of ingredients with boiled rice and you have a piping hot, seductively fragrant dish. When eaten for breakfast, it warms your whole body, making a great start to an active day.

Ingredients
- stock   500g
  (cooked with pork and old hen)
- dory fish   200g
- preserved vegetables   50g
- pork   100g
- cooked rice   200g
- salt   5g
- spring onion   5g
- ginger   5g
- yellow wine   20g
- MSG   2g

Preparation

1. Dice the pork finely. Remove all bones from the fish, leaving only the flesh. Dice the fish, stir-fry with salt, yellow wine and MSG. Dice the preserved vegetables and spring onions. Cut the ginger into shreds. 2. Boil the stock. Add the rice, fish and pork. When it has boiled, sprinkle on preserved vegetables, spring onions and ginger. Stir and serve.

Variations

RICE IN VEGETABLE SOUP – Cut small green vegetables into pieces. Dice dried mushrooms and cured meat. Stir-fry all the above, and add cooking wine and water. Pour in cooked rice. Bring it to a boil, then add salt and chicken essence to taste.

RICE IN MUSHROOM AND BAMBOO SHOOT SOUP – Dice dried mushrooms, bamboo shoots and yam. Cut chye sim (Chinese flowering cabbage) into small pieces. Stir-fry all the above. Add cooked rice, water, salt and MSG. Boil and serve.

龍蝦湯雲吞 (long2 xia1 tang1 yun2 tun1)

WONTON IN LOBSTER SOUP

The lobster soup has a beautiful, cheery red colour, and you can smell the lobster succulence from a mile away. This Western soup is a perfect fit with Chinese wontons, making it extra divine.

Ingredients

• lobster	1	• fresh cream	40g
• wonton skin	240g	• onion	20g
• pork loin	200g	• milk	100g
• salt	5g	• stock	100g
• corn starch	5g	(cooked with pork and old hen)	
• egg	1	• flour	100g
• pepper	2g	• cooking wine	10g
• tomato	50g		

Preparation

1. Cut open the lobster's head, and remove the shell. Using a blender, churn the pork into a paste, and do the same for the lobster. Mix both pastes with salt, corn starch, egg and cooking wine. Stir in a constant direction till springy, and you have the filling. Wrap into the wonton skins. Boil the wontons till they float. 2. Dice the onion. Skin and mash the tomato. Heat a wok, put in 10g of cream and stir-fry the onion till fragrant. Pan-fry the lobster head and shell for a while. Pour in milk and 20g stock, cook for 2 minutes, remove the lobster parts, and sieve. This is your soup. 3. Take another pot, pour in 30g cream and flour. Stir-fry and blend on low heat. Add the remaining stock, tomato and the soup above. Boil on medium heat. Turn off the fire and sieve. Place the wontons in, sprinkle on some pepper, and serve.

上海小馄饨 (shang4 hai2 xiao3 hun2 tun4)

SHANGHAI DUMPLINGS

Shanghai Dumplings are small and dainty, made with a thin skin and a
succulent filling. Usually, a flavourful soup comes together with the dumplings.
The dish is a common sight in Shanghai night markets, especially in winter.

Ingredients

•	small dumpling skins	10
•	pork	40g
•	chicken soup	600g
•	pepper	5g
•	salt	3g
•	cooking wine	5g
•	spring onion	3g
•	prawn shell	
•	seaweed	

Preparation

1. Dice the pork into a paste. Mix in salt and cooking wine for the filling. Wrap into the skins, and
pinch the skins such that they resemble goldfish tails. Cook in boiling water. 2. Dice spring onions,
prawn shells and seaweed, and sprinkle into heated chicken soup. Place the dumplings in and serve.
You can add some more seaweed and prawn shells to taste.

豆腐雞鴨血湯 (dou4 fu ji1 ya1 xue3 tang1)

TOFU DUCK BLOOD SOUP

Tofu Duck Blood Soup is frequently sold in roadside stalls. It is easy to prepare and extremely tasty. Moreover, duck blood contains high levels of iron, making it good for the blood.

Ingredients

- tofu   100g
- congealed chicken and duck blood   100g
- salt   5g
- chicken essence   5g
- pepper   3g
- sesame oil   3g
- spring onion   5g

Preparation

1. Cut the congealed chicken and duck blood and tofu into small pieces. Cook the blood, tofu, salt, chicken essence and pepper in water. 2. Sprinkle on sesame oil and diced spring onions after boiling. Serve.

Variations

TOFU DUCK BLOOD SOUP WITH SPINACH
– Wash, cut spinach into pieces. Blanch spinach, and add into the above soup after boiling.
TOFU DUCK BLOOD SOUP WITH
VERMICELLI – Prepare as above. Add some rice vermicelli into the soup after boiling. Boil again and serve.

皮蛋瘦肉粥 (pi2 dan4 shou4 rou4 zhou1)
PORRIDGE WITH PORK AND CENTURY EGG

Easy to prepare, this bowl of tasty Porridge with Pork and Century Egg will warm you when the weather turns cold.

Ingredients

• rice	150g
• century eggs	3
• lean pork	150g
• sesame oil	3g
• salt	5g
• spring onion	2g
• ginger	2g

Preparation

1. Wash the rice. Add 5g water, sesame oil, salt. Mix and soak for 30 minutes. Cut the ginger into shreds. Dice the spring onion and century eggs. Cut the pork into rectangular slices, and add a little salt. Mix and marinate for about 20 minutes. 2. Boil water on high heat. Blanch the pork, and scoop away the bubbles. Add strips of ginger and half the century eggs after boiling. Let the soup boil again, and wait 1 to 2 minutes. Pour in the rice and stir as you do so. Let it boil again. Switch to low heat and cook for 40 minutes. Stir continuously to prevent the rice from sticking to the pot. Pour in the rest of the century eggs, and cook for another 10 minutes. Sprinkle in the spring onion and serve.

Variations

SHREDDED PORK PORRIDGE – Take tender pork loin, and cut into thin strips. Stir-fry with oil, ginger, spring onion and cooking wine. Cook some porridge. Add the pork, salt and MSG to taste. Boil and serve.

五香豆腐乾茶葉蛋 (wu3 xiang1 dou4 fu gan1 cha2 ye4 dan4)
"FIVE SPICES" TEA EGGS WITH DRIED TOFU

"Five Spices" Tea Eggs with Dried Tofu is a well-known traditional Shanghai snack and its origins can be traced back to as early as the Qing dynasty. The eggs and dried tofu are cooked in ingredients like tea leaves, cinnamon peel and cumin, and thus give off a multi-layered fragrance, earning its name as "five spices".

Ingredients

•	egg	2500g
•	coarse (uncooked) tea leaves	75g
•	soy sauce	400g
•	sugar	10g
•	cumin	30g
•	cinnamon peel	20g
•	mandarin orange peel	20g
•	salt	15g
•	cooking wine	50g
•	dried tofu	800g

Preparation

1. Wash the eggs, cook in a pot till half-done, and plop them into cold water immediately. Shell the eggs. Place the dried tofu and eggs into a pot. 2. Wrap cumin, cinnamon peel, mandarin orange peel, soy sauce, salt, cooking wine and sugar in a gauze, and place in the pot. Pour in water till it covers all the ingredients. 3. Cover the pot and boil on high heat. Switch to low heat and stew for 30 minutes. Turn down to extremely low heat and stew for half a day. Turn off the fire, leaving the eggs and tofu in the stew, till you wish to serve them.

雙丸湯 (shuang1 wan2 tang1)

FISH AND BEEF BALL SOUP

This is a soup with a base bursting with the flavours of smooth delicate fishballs and chewy, springy beef balls.

Ingredients

- beef   250g
- fish flesh   250g
- starch   16g
- chicken essence   2g
- salt   10g
- coriander   3g

Preparation

1. Dice the beef into a paste. Add water, 5g salt and 8g starch. Continue to stir in the same direction till it becomes springy. Do the same with the fish flesh. 2. Grab a handful of paste, squeeze between your thumb and index finger to make a ball, and drop the ball into a pot of water. Repeat till both pastes are finished. Add chicken essence and cook the balls on low heat. When done, add in cut coriander and serve.

Variations

FISH AND BEEF BALL SOUP WITH CRAB MUSHROOMS – Prepare as above, adding washed crab mushrooms when the fish and beef balls are nearly cooked. Cook all till done and serve.

FISH AND BEEF BALL SOUP WITH SEAWEED AND VERMICELLI – Prepare as above, adding in vermicelli when the balls are nearly cooked. Cook all till done and serve with small pieces of seaweed.

蓮藕栗子芡实羹 (lian2 ou3 li4 zi qian4 shi2 geng1)
STEW OF LOTUS SEEDS, CHESTNUTS AND GORGON FRUIT

A bowl of this delightful stew helps remove excess heat and nourishes your skin without sacrificing taste.

Ingredients
- lotus seeds   15g
- gorgon fruit   50g
- honey   10g
- chestnuts   10g

Preparation
1. Wash and slice the lotus seeds. Cook with gorgon fruit, chestnuts and water for an hour. 2. When the stew cools slightly, add the honey and serve.

甜
点

DESSERT
DIM SUM

赤豆什果冰 (chi4 dou4 shi2 guo3 bing1)

FRUIT ICE WITH RED BEANS

Fruit Ice with Red Beans is a dessert recommended for the summer. It has an ice-cold sensation that soothes your throat and revitalising vitamins in the fruits.

Ingredients

- red beans   400g
- agar-agar   50g
- white sugar   100g
- condensed milk   100g
- starfruit   50g
- watermelon   100g
- cantaloupe   50g
- pomelo   20g

Preparation

1. Wash the red beans and soak them in water overnight till they burst open. Boil them with water in a pot, then cook on low heat till they become a paste. Add in the sugar and agar-agar, stirring on low heat for a short while. Turn off the fire and pour the sweet soup into bowls to cool, then refrigerate it for later use. 2. Using a scoop, make balls of watermelon. Slice the starfruit and cantaloupe, and remove the skin from the pomelo sacs. Crush some ice cubes with a crusher machine, blend in the red bean soup and scoop into bowls, adding the fruits and condensed milk on top.

赤豆雪花糕 (chi4 dou4 xue3 hua1 gao1)

SNOW CAKES WITH RED BEANS

Snow Cakes with Red Beans are made with red beans and almond tofu. They are sweet, soft and tasty, offering two distinctly different textures and tastes.

Ingredients

- red beans   500g
- glutinous rice   200g
- agar-agar   50g
- fresh milk   500ml
- fresh cream   50g
- almond juice   20g
- sugar   200g

Preparation

1. Wash the red beans and glutinous rice, then soak in water overnight. After the red beans have burst open, boil them with glutinous rice in a pot. Then cook on low heat till the glutinous rice and red beans are totally blended, and thick enough to stick on the scoop. Add in sugar, stir and turn off the fire. Pour the sweet soup into moulds and allow it to cool, only filling two-thirds of the moulds. When cooled, refrigerate the soup. 2. Boil the milk and fresh cream and add in sugar and agar-agar. Cook and stir till the sugar and agar-agar have dissolved completely, then turn off the fire. Add in the almond juice and mix, then pour the mixture into the moulds on top of the red bean soup. Refrigerate till the almond soup has solidified, then serve.

赤豆圓子羹 (chi4 dou4 yuan2 zi3 geng1)
RED BEAN RICEBALL STEW

Red Bean Riceball Stew is a traditional Shanghai snack. Red beans are high in phosphorus and iron, and are good for the body in summer and winter.

Ingredients
- red beans   250g
- small glutinous rice balls   100g
- sugar   20g

Preparation

1. Clean the red beans thoroughly, boil in water, then stew them into a paste on low heat. 2. Mix a little warm water into the glutinous rice flour. Using your hands, knead into a dough that does not stick to the hands, yet also does not break apart. Then knead the dough into long thin sticks. Dice them with a knife, then hand-roll them into balls. Sprinkle some glutinous flour onto the riceballs, so they don't stick together. 3. Put the riceballs into the red bean stew, and heat till they float on the surface. Add a little water and bring the stew to a boil again. Add sugar, stir and serve in bowls.

桂花玫瑰凍 (gui4 hua1 mei3 gui1 dong4)

OSMANTHUS ROSE JELLY

Osmanthus Rose Jelly is an exquisite-looking dish with translucent osmanthus-flavoured jelly. It has the refreshing smell of light osmanthus fragrance, and is very popular as a dessert.

Ingredients

- osmanthus tea   40g
- rose syrup   30g
- konyaku jelly   20g
- honey   60g
- agar-agar   50g
- fresh milk   500ml
- cream   50g
- sugar   100g
- icing sugar   40g

Preparation

1. Boil the milk and cream, add in sugar and agar-agar, and stir till they are completely dissolved. Turn off the fire, then stir in the rose syrup and pour the mixture into square moulds, only filling half of the moulds. Refrigerate the moulds till the jelly solidifies. 2. Make the osmanthus tea with boiling water, making it thick. Mix the jelly powder and icing sugar and stir the mixture into the tea, then add honey. Heat on low heat, and turn off the heat after the tea boils. 3. Pour the tea syrup into the square moulds, and then freeze. Once the tea syrup solidifies, remove from the moulds and serve.

黑芝麻湯圓 (hei1 zhi1 ma2 tang1 yuan2)

BLACK SESAME BALLS

Black Sesame Balls have a long history and is a unique dessert from China. It is very popular during Chinese festivals.

Ingredients
- glutinous rice flour   300g
- black sesame   300g
- sugar   150g
- lard   50g

Preparation
1. Stir-fry the black sesame till done, then crush it. For every 2 parts of sesame, blend in 1 part lard and 2 parts sugar. Roll into balls weighing about 10g each. This will later be the filling for your riceballs. 2. Adding water, knead the glutinous rice flour into dough. The dough should not stick to your fingers, and should neither be too hard nor too soft. Roll into long sticks, then chop into small pieces with a knife. 3. Roll each small piece into a ball, then use your thumb to make a depression on top. Put in the ball of filling, then use your fingers to slowly close up the hole on top, and lightly roll the ball in your palm to make it rounder. The finished balls should be about as big as a hawthorn berry. Boil some water and throw in the balls. Once they float up to the surface, they are ready to be served.

Variations
LOTUS PASTE BALLS – Prepare ingredients as above, but substitute the sesame with lotus paste. Wrap into the skin and cook.
RED BEAN PASTE BALLS – Prepare ingredients as above, but substitute the sesame with red bean paste. Wrap into the skin and cook.

紅豆糕 (hong2 dou4 gao1)

RED BEAN CAKES

These soft and sticky Red Bean Cakes are made of interlacing layers of glutinous rice and red bean paste. Easy to make, this lovely dessert is perfect for culinary novices.

Ingredients

• red beans	1000g
• glutinous rice	500g
• soft white sugar	500g
• lard	200g

Preparation

1. Wash the red beans and glutinous rice, and soak in water overnight. Setting aside a small bowl for red beans, pour the rest into a pot and boil with water, then cook on low heat till all the beans burst. 2. Sieve the red bean skins out, then pour everything into a gauze bag, squeezing out as much water as you can. What you are left with is a red bean paste. Melt the lard in a wok, then add in the bean paste and sugar. Stir-fry till the bean paste sticks to your scoop. 3. Steam the glutinous rice for about 40 minutes, then pour onto wet gauze and dab on cool water. Knead it till it becomes a paste, then add in the bowl of red beans set aside earlier. Knead some more, till the red beans are evenly distributed throughout. 4. Place a thin layer of bean paste at the bottom of a mould, then a layer of glutinous rice on top, then a layer of bean paste, then another layer of glutinous rice. Press it all down tight. Steam in the steamer on high heat for 10 minutes. Repeat for all the other cakes. When the cakes have cooled, remove from the moulds and serve.

紅豆西米糕 (hong2 dou4 xi1 mi3 gao1)
RED BEAN SAGO CAKES

Red Bean Sago Cakes are made differently from most desserts. The sago needs
to be cooked thoroughly and spread evenly into the mould for a chewy texture.

Ingredients

- sweet tapioca "pearls"   200g
- red bean paste filing   500g
- sago   400g

Preparation

1. Boil water in a pot, cook the "pearls" in it till they float on the surface and turn translucent, and
scoop them out for later use. 2. Wash the sago and soak it in water for about half an hour, then
spread a 0.5cm layer of sago in the mould. Pour red bean paste into the mould, filling it up with
another layer of sago at the end. Repeat for the other cakes. Place into a steamer, and steam on high
heat for 10 minutes, then on low heat for 10 minutes. When the cakes have cooled, remove them
from the moulds and sprinkle "pearls" around them.

紅豆鑽 (hong2 dou4 zuan1)

RED BEAN DIAMONDS

Red Bean Diamonds are incredibly transparent and shiny. They combine fine red bean paste, "pearls" and condensed milk for a smooth and intensely tasty dessert, with a bit of a chewy texture.

Ingredients

• red beans	500g
• sugar	100g
• condensed milk	50g
• sweet tapioca "pearls"	200g

Preparation

1. Boil water in a pot, cook the "pearls" in it till they float on the surface and turn translucent, and scoop them out for later use. 2. Wash the red beans and boil in a pot, then steam on low heat for half an hour till the red beans become mushy. Sieve the skins out, crush the skins in a crusher machine, and add into the paste again. Stew on low heat till the paste becomes sticky, stir in sugar and refrigerate. 3. Before serving, add in the "pearls" and condensed milk.

紅棗荔枝糖水 (hong2 zao3 li4 zhi1 tang2 shui3)

RED DATE LYCHEE SWEET SOUP

Red dates and lychees are known for their skin-nourishing properties, and are hence popular with women. This dish is a very authentic Cantonese dessert, and it tastes mildly sweet and refreshingly cool.

Ingredients
- red dates   100g
- fresh dates   500g
- lotus seeds   50g
- brown sugar   50g

Preparation
1. Wash the lotus seeds and soak in water for 2 hours. Then put them into a pot, together with washed red dates, peeled and seeded lychee, water and brown sugar. 2. Boil on high heat, then on low heat for half an hour. Cool and serve.

酒釀圓子 (jiu3 niang4 yuan2 zi3)
GLUTINOUS RICEBALLS WITH WINE LEES

Glutinous Riceballs with Wine Lees is a famous snack from Shanghai. The riceballs are soft and sticky, yet chewy and bouncy at the same time. The wine lees have an intense sour-sweet flavour and the light fragrance of osmanthus.

Ingredients

•	select glutinous rice	1000g
•	sugar	200g
•	sweet wine lees	500g
•	sugar osmanthus	10g

Preparation

1. Wash the glutinous rice and soak for 1 hour in cold water. Wash and drain, then crush with a stone mortar and pestle. Sieve the rice in a 10-mesh sieve, and you have the flour for the riceballs. 2. Using a flat bamboo plate with holes, mix the flour with water. In your right hand, use a wet brush to sprinkle water evenly into the flour. In your left hand, hold the plate and keep pushing it forward. The flour will curdle into balls that will gradually get bigger until it forms small balls of about 1cm in diameter. 3. Allow boiled water to cool before adding into the wine lees. Beat them with a pair of chopsticks till they become wine lees soup. Boil water in a pot, cook the riceballs till done, then add in the wine lees soup. Add sugar and sugar osmanthus, then serve in bowls together with the soup.

蜜柚蛋花露 (mi4 you4 dan4 hua1 lu4)
HONEY YUZU EGG DROP NECTAR

Yuzu tea is a very popular dessert, with its mixture of sweet and sour flavour. Making it into an egg drop nectar not only preserves its unique taste, but also integrates the flavour of eggs.

Ingredients

- yuzu tea   100g
- egg   1
- honey   20g

Preparation

1. Beat the egg and pour into boiling water. Stir till the egg solidifies into wisps, and turn off the fire. 2. Put the egg wisps into a bowl, mix in yuzu tea and honey, and serve.

木瓜牛奶 (mu4 gua1 niu2 nai3)

PAPAYA MILK

Papayas are known as "the breast-enhancing fruit", which contain large amounts of micro-vitamins. Papaya milk has a mild fruit taste, and its flavour is even better when chilled.

Ingredients
- milk   500g
- papaya   200g
- solid green bean soup   200g
- sugar   30g

Preparation
1. Wash the papaya, remove the skin and seeds, and cut into small pieces. Cook with water till done, and set aside for later use. 2. Remove the green bean soup from the packaging, cut into pieces, and set aside for later use. 3. Heat the milk in a microwave, then add it the papaya, green bean soup and sugar. Blend well and serve.

西米南瓜烤布丁 (xi1 mi3 nan2 gua1 kao3 bu4 ding1)
ROASTED SAGO PUMPKIN PUDDING

Roasted Sago Pumpkin Pudding has a fragrant and sweet flavour without being too overpowering, and is great as an after-meal dessert.

Ingredients

• egg	2
• honey	20g
• milk	400ml
• sago	300g
• pumpkin	100g
• cream	100g

Preparation

1. Wash the sago and cook in boiling water, remember to keep stirring lest the sago sticks to the pot. Remove the sago once it becomes translucent. Boil another pot of water and cook the sago in it till it becomes totally transparent, then pour the water away. 2. Skin and dice the pumpkin and set aside for later use. 3. Heat the oven to 150°C. Beat the egg and honey, add in milk and blend thoroughly. Pour the mixture into several baking cups brushed with butter. Add the pumpkin and sago in the cups and seal with foil. 4. Put the baking cups into a baking pan, and place another cup of warm water in the pan. Bake for about 10 minutes, open the seals, then bake for another 5 to 8 minutes. The pudding is now ready to be served.

西米糕 (xi1 mi3 gao1)

SAGO CAKES

Sago Cakes have a snowy-white and translucent skin with yellow peanut
bits that make the cakes look irresistible.

Ingredients

- rice flour   160g
- sugar   140g
- sago   30g
- coconut milk   100g
- peanut bits   30g

Preparation

1. Mix the coconut milk with 1/4 cup of water, then add in the rice flour and mix everything into a
thin paste. Then slowly pour in 1 cup of water and sugar, and blend thoroughly. 2. Wash the sago
and cook in water till translucent, then wash in cold water. Mix the sago into the rice paste, and
pour the paste into pre-heated small balls. Steam in a steamer for 6 minutes. When the cakes have
cooled, remove from the bowls and add peanut bits beside them. Serve.

Variations

RED BEAN CRYSTAL CAKES – Prepare rice
flour, glutinous rice flour, wheat flour, and
sugar. Cook red beans in water till they become
mushy, and drain. Sieve the flours and mix into
a paste with water. Boil and add sugar. Pour into
small bowls, add the red beans, and steam on
high heat till done.

PINEAPPLE CRYSTAL CAKES – Prepare the
basic ingredients, together with fresh pineapple.
Cut the pineapple flesh into pieces, place with
sago into small bowls, and steam till done.

HAWTHORN CRYSTAL CAKES – Prepare the
basic ingredients together with fresh hawthorn
fruits. Skin the fruits and cut into pieces, place
with sago into small bowls, and steam till done.

香芒糯米卷 (xiang1 mang2 nuo4 mi3 juan3)

MANGO GLUTINOUS RICE ROLLS

Mango Glutinous Rice Rolls are sour, with a little bit of sweetness, and tightly packed with fresh mango bits hidden inside these soft and sticky rolls.

Ingredients

- glutinous rice flour   150g
- corn flour   50g
- sugar   80g
- mangoes   700g
- desiccated coconut   100g
- egg   1
- cheese powder   20g
- gelatin powder   10g
- milk   200ml

Preparation

1. Mix the glutinous rice flour, corn flour and sugar, then pour onto a tray. The tray should first be covered with baking paper and brushed with a thin layer of oil. Steam the tray and its contents on high heat for 10 minutes, till the glutinous rice flour solidifies. 2. Mix the egg yolk, sugar, cheese powder, cornstarch powder, gelatin powder, milk and water, and heat till the mixture thickens and bubbles like molten magma. Remove the yellow mixture from heat and let it cool. 3. Skin and seed the mangoes, and cut the flesh into strips for later use. 4. Slide the glutinous rice flour and baking paper off the tray, and knead into a thin skin. Spread the yellow mixture on, then sprinkle with desiccated coconut and lay the mango strips on top. Roll up the skin and sprinkle more coconut on top. Place the rolls, still in the baking paper, in the freezer for an hour, then slice and serve.

香芋椰果露 (xiang1 yu4 ye1 guo3 lu4)

YAM COCONUT NECTAR

Yam has a texture that is a cross between that of potato and chestnut. It is mildly sweet and fragrant, and carries with it a strong pleasant aftertaste. It is also very nutritious, and unique in colour, fragrance and taste, making it perfect as an ingredient for desserts.

Ingredients

• coconut jelly	50g
• yam	500g
• coconut juice	250ml

Preparation

1. Wash the yams and steam for about 25 minutes in a steamer. After they have cooled slightly, skin and cut into small pieces for later use. 2. Pour the coconut juice into a bowl, heat in a microwave for 2 minutes, then add in the yams and coconut jelly. Stir and serve.

椰絲卷 (ye1 si1 juan3)
SHREDDED COCONUT ROLLS

Shredded Coconut Rolls remind one of Hainan. The egg rolls are slightly savoury, yet covered with a sweet sauce, combining the two into an unforgettable taste.

Ingredients
- eggs   4
- flour   200g
- sugar   100g
- salt   20g
- shredded coconut   100g
- milk   300ml
- chestnut powder   100g

Preparation
1. Beat an egg, add flour, sugar and chestnut powder. Stir and heat till the mixture becomes thick. Set aside for later use. 2. Beat the rest of the eggs, then stir in flour, sugar and salt one by one. Heat a flat-bottomed saucepan, lightly brushed with cooking oil, then pour in the eggs. While cooking, keep shaking the saucepan so that the eggs are evenly spread on the bottom. When the bottom has solidified, flip the omelet and fry for a while more. 3. Put the omelet into a plate, brush on the sauce you made earlier, roll up and slice. Cover with shredded coconut and serve.

银耳炖木瓜 (yin2 er3 dun4 mu4 gua1)
WHITE FUNGUS STEWED WITH PAPAYA

White Fungus Stewed with Papaya is a nutritious dessert for the skin
and body. Frequent consumption nourishes the lungs, beautifes the skin,
prevents premature wrinkles, and keeps the skin smooth and tender.

Ingredients

• white Jew's ear fungus	20g
• papaya	200g
• almond	20g
• rock sugar	10g

Preparation

1. Soak the fungus in water till it softens, then wash. 2. Skin and seed the papaya, then cut into small pieces. 3. Remove the covering of the almonds, wash and put into a stew pot with the fungus and rock sugar. Add some water and cook for 30 minutes. Serve with the papayas.

檸檬蜜枣 (ning2 meng2 mi4 zao3)

LEMON WITH SWEET DATES

Lemon with Sweet Dates tastes sweet and sour. The dates contain all sorts of vitamins and can be stored for a long time, making them especially appropriate for winter.

Ingredients
- red dates   300g
- lemon   30g
- honey   500g

Preparation
1. Wash and slice the lemon, soak in honey and leave in a cool and covered place for a week.
2. Wash the red dates and steam on medium heat for 10 minutes. Then put them into the same pot of honey, leave for 2 days, remove and serve.

Variations
GOLDEN SILK DATES – Prepare some golden silk dates, lotus seeds, ginger, honey, salt and sesame oil. Steam the dates with shredded ginger till done. Put the sesame oil, honey, cooked lotus seeds and salt into a pot, and stir over heat. Pour in the dates, stir and serve.

龟苓膏什果拼 (gui1 ling2 gao1 shi2 guo3 pin1)
TORTOISE JELLY WITH ASSORTED FRUITS

Tortoise Jelly with Assorted Fruits is an easy dish to make, and you can even choose the fruits you like and mix them in. A cup of this in the summer refreshes and cools you.

Ingredients

•	tortoise jelly powder	200g
•	honey	30g
•	watermelon	200g
•	mango	200g
•	coconut jelly	100g

Preparation

1. Pour some tortoise jelly powder into a bowl, pour in warm water and stir into a paste. Add honey to reduce the bitterness. Add in boiling water and stir, or heat over a fire and stir. Pour out and cool, then refrigerate. After it has solidified, dice and put aside for later use. 2. Using a fruit scoop, make several watermelon balls. Skin and seed the mangoes, and cut into small pieces for later use. 3. Take your glass cutlery, spread some ice cubes on the bottom, then add in the tortoise jelly, watermelon balls, mangoes and coconut jelly, and the dessert is ready to serve.

Index

Acknowledgements

We would like to thank the following establishments for their help with the dim sum preparation in this book.

上海新旺餐饮管理有限公司
Shanghai Xin Wang F&B Management Co.,Ltd

一茶一坐
Chamate

上海齐鲁万怡大酒店
Courtyard by Marriott Shanghai - Pudong

上海屋里香
Shanghai Wu Li Xiang Restaurant

上海城隍庙小吃
Shanghai Cheng Huang Miao Snack

上海悦亭
Shanghai Yue Ting Restaurant

北京护国寺小吃
Beijing Hu Guo Si Snack

山东潍坊金茂国际大酒店有限公司
Weifang Hotel MontRiche International Group

福州泰福楼
Fuzhou Tai Fu Lou Restaurant

盐城洪祥大酒店
Yancheng Hong Xiang Restaurant